the power of
EQ

the power of
EQ

Stronger leadership
through emotional intelligence

KAREN D. NUTTER

Certified Master Coach

Published by Advantage, Charleston, South Carolina.
Member of Advantage Media Group.

ADVANTAGE is a registered trademark and the Advantage colophon is a trademark of Advantage Media Group, Inc.

Printed in the United States of America.

ISBN: 978-1-59932-603-0
LCCN: 2015942305

This publication is designed to provide accurate and authoritative information in regard to the subject matter covered. It is sold with the understanding that the publisher is not engaged in rendering legal, accounting, or other professional services. If legal advice or other expert assistance is required, the services of a competent professional person should be sought.

Advantage Media Group is proud to be a part of the Tree Neutral® program. Tree Neutral offsets the number of trees consumed in the production and printing of this book by taking proactive steps such as planting trees in direct proportion to the number of trees used to print books. To learn more about Tree Neutral, please visit **www.treeneutral.com**. To learn more about Advantage's commitment to being a responsible steward of the environment, please visit **www.advantagefamily.com/green**

Advantage Media Group is a publisher of business, self-improvement, and professional development books and online learning. We help entrepreneurs, business leaders, and professionals share their Stories, Passion, and Knowledge to help others Learn & Grow. Do you have a manuscript or book idea that you would like us to consider for publishing? Please visit **advantagefamily.com** or call **1.866.775.1696.**

Acknowledgments

The desire to write this book has been brewing inside of me for some time. But the inspiration to act on that impulse came from many different people who have impacted my life at various stages along the way. I would like to acknowledge them for all they have given me.

My friend Cathy and my Aunt Anne, who have always shown *self-awareness* and *empathy* through their kindness, friendship, and love.

My friend and colleague Teri, who gave me a chance years ago professionally and still believes in me today and encouraged me to "write a book."

My friend Peggy McGuinness, for using her editing expertise to help me with this book.

My son Josh, who gives me unconditional love and respect! He's the apple of my eye and has shown me firsthand that having a passion to follow your dream pays off because he followed his passion, and he gave me the nerve to follow mine. Thank you for that and for giving me a daughter through marriage, Quincy, who also followed her dream through dolphin research. Together, you live a passion-filled life professionally and personally.

All my clients who keep me going and challenge me professionally and personally with *self-regulation* by saying things like, "I hired you because you walk the walk." Now, that's pressure to maintain!

My grandfather Ettore who was "my rock," and my Mother who showed me a good work ethic, social skills, and motivation. My mother would always say, "You can do anything you put your mind to." Without her, I might have given up!

Table of Contents

Introduction

DISCOVERING MY EQ

Years ago, when I was working in a thriving sales career, I started to become ill but tried to ignore it. I saw numerous doctors and tried a variety of medicines, natural supplements, and therapies, but I didn't get better. Instead, my illness got worse, and I ended up spending several years in bed, recuperating.

While in the recuperation period, I realized part of my issue was that, although I was very good at my profession, it was draining the energy out of me. I came to realize, just because I excelled at my job, that didn't mean it was healthy for me, nor aligned with my passion and natural calling. As I worked on my healing and analyzed my life, I came to realize that my natural calling was leading people to a better life, not chasing businesses and trying to make sales, as I had been doing. Reviewing my own Emotional Intelligence (EQ) assessment also validated for me that being a coach and facilitator of groups is what makes the best use of my God-given talents.

I decided to go back to school and focus on health and wellness. That decision led me to a position where I provided guidance to people wanting to change their health habits, which then led me to becoming a coach and Master Coach Trainer. I've had intensive training and experience in intrinsic coaching, identifying and analyzing internal motivators, behavioral analysis, neurolinguistic training, and more. I've received many awards, but the two I'm proudest of are my Business Network International Member of the

Year Award and the Frank Wellness Barker Award. Both mean so much to me because they come from my community in Jacksonville, Florida. I'm also included as one of the best coaches in the world in Joseph Smart's book, *Interviews with Senior Successful Coaches.*

I am happy to say that I am now healthy and in a profession that is aligned with my passion, my natural abilities, and my true calling. It has allowed me freedom and excitement each and every day and a feeling of peace like I've never had before. This kind of contentment in life is possible for everyone, and I thrive on helping people find success in their personal and professional lives!

Whether you're an individual searching for solutions or a business leader looking to empower your employees to create success for themselves and your business, I would like to work with you to help you create the life you deserve. I want to help you find balance in an unbalanced world!

CHAPTER 1

Leadership and Emotional Intelligence: Tell Me How I Can Help

LEADERSHIP MATTERS

Strong leadership in a corporation is so important because what happens at the top always funnels down. For all parts of a corporation to work well, leadership needs to start at the top. Leaders must have a strong work ethic, commitment to the organization, and consistency, and they definitely need to feel empathy for their employees.

That's why emotional intelligence is important. Although it's wonderful to have leaders with a high IQ and the skills to develop the company, it's even more important to have leaders with high emotional intelligence. Leaders with high emotional intelligence invite a high level of collaboration and productivity, starting with management but including all workers, all the way down to the janitor. When that happens, the company has cohesiveness and camaraderie. People are excited to go to work.

People with a high IQ are book smart but not always people smart, not always self-aware or aware of how their words and actions affect others. While high IQ is wonderful and having paper credentials is great, they alone will not inspire and encourage the cohesiveness required for a successful team. Sometimes the very intelligent and highly educated people among us just don't know how to implement their knowledge or demonstrate it so that they can be role models. That is where EQ can save the day. People with high EQ are more empathetic and open and more willing to listen. They are able to communicate their knowledge in a way that encourages others to express themselves. This approach invites all the employees and the management team to want to be more creative, to want to be more a part of the team. And because it invites their thoughts, innovative ideas can come out.

John Maxwell, a top management guru, says, "Spend time listening to others, and let them impress you. And by doing that, you've automatically gotten their respect." When a leader listens to everyone's ideas, everyone feels they have made a contribution, and it's a win-win situation for the leader, too. Even if someone's idea ends up not being used, that individual is validated as an important contributor toward the final solution or action.

WHAT IS EMOTIONAL INTELLIGENCE?

Emotional intelligence, often abbreviated as EQ or EI, is the ability to sense, understand, and effectively apply the power and acumen of emotions to facilitate high levels of collaboration and productivity. Emotional intelligence is awareness of your own emotions and those of others. Unlike IQ, EQ can be learned and, with practice, will increase over time.

Ninety percent of the difference between star performers and average performers in senior leadership is emotional intelligence. People with high emotional intelligence are generally consistent, level headed, and on an even keel. They're not constantly battling their own negative thoughts. Having an MBA in and of itself is not enough to be a good leader. You need EQ so you can understand your family, your customers, your coworkers, and your own boss. With EQ, you know how to manage expectations and you know how to ultimately meet the needs of your employees. The more transparent and vulnerable leaders are, the more authentic and positive the whole environment feels. I truly believe the best words a leader can use are "Tell me how I can help." Only a leader with the self-awareness and empathy of an emotionally intelligence person can say that and follow through.

EQ TIES IT ALL TOGETHER

EQ is what ties all the elements of leadership together. It's not enough to score high in only some aspects of emotional intelligence. Let's say you're a good listener, you've got a lot of expertise, and you've got a good attitude. You're heading in the right direction, but if you want to become a better leader, you need more—maybe more motivation or better social skills. Everybody, even the most natural leader, has areas of emotional intelligence that are stronger than others. Your natural skills are a good starting point for working on the other aspects of emotional intelligence. When you get it all together, as I hope this book will help you to do, your weaker areas will be stronger, and your strong areas will be even better. You'll be ready to be a more effective leader.

LEADERSHIP AND PRODUCTIVITY

Leaders with high EQ promote productivity through collaboration. When people feel part of a group or feel listened to, they will then be more productive. When a friend just listens to you, you feel energized and ready to move forward, even if the friend didn't offer any practical ideas. She didn't have a solution for you, but being listened to helped you find your own solution.

In my practice, I've found that someone who comes for a coaching session just wants to be heard. There are times when I can be most helpful by simply nodding and saying, "Tell me more about that." The client leaves feeling great. And what happened? He was listened to—and now he has a bounce in his step for the rest of the day.

Leaders who listen well to the team are, by definition, open to new ideas and collaboration. That's the key to higher productivity. When employees feel valued, they're willing to work harder. They don't call in sick as much, and they don't watch the clock. They like their work and want to succeed at it.

RETAINING AND NURTURING TALENT

Leaders with high EQ are very good at retaining and nurturing talent. They can improve productivity substantially, simply by making good people want to stay with the company.

Listening skills are important, but consistency is key here. When a leader is consistent in every aspect, people feel comfortable. It's much like parenting. Experts in parenting emphasize consistency: Have a normal bedtime, have a regular breakfast time, have a regular lunchtime, have the same rules, and ensure punishment for breaking the rules is in proportion to the offense committed. As a result, the child feels secure and feels like showing up and being part of the family.

The same is true in an organization. When the leadership displays consistency and expects pretty much the same from everybody, while treating everybody as an individual, it invites more productivity in a nurturing environment. And it retains the talent, so you don't have to worry about the talent looking elsewhere. At the same time, the talent wants to give you their best effort.

Strong leadership retains the clients as well. When the employees feel good about being at work, when they feel nurtured and happy in their jobs, it shows with the clients. The clients hear that enthusiasm, they hear that passion, and they know that the employee will do whatever it takes to get the job done for them. When a customer says to an employee, "You do such a great job," and the employee responds, "Well, I work for the greatest boss in the world," that's a client who's going to stay with you.

In my previous career, I had a boss who was a true leader. When I was a young single parent in sales, my car needed new tires. Now, I was making enough that I could have bought my own tires, but finding the time was hard. My boss said to me, "Take an hour and go down to the tire store and put it on our credit card." That felt like a gift from heaven—it made me feel valued. It wasn't that I couldn't afford it; it was that he thought enough of an employee to say, "Let's do this for her."

As a result of that, I told several of our clients, "Guess what happened the other day, guess what my boss did." So what does that do? That creates goodwill for me, and it makes the clients feel good. They think, *Wow, that's a great company.* It makes them want to stay around because they feel, *Look how well he treats his employees; that must mean he'll treat us well, too.*

I once had a manager who was a model of consistency and good leadership. She was great at treating us all with respect. She was also a really good listener during meetings. She didn't dominate; she let us all have our input. Of course, she then made the decision. Even when we didn't like her final decision, because she valued our input, we felt valued and went along with it with full team support.

She was also a very good manager because she treated us all fairly and was very consistent with rewards. She knew how to make us feel appreciated. If you gave a good presentation or brought in a new client, you could be sure there would be a note on your desk saying, "Great job, way to go," along with some little gift. So we knew, just like children know, "If you do something good, you're going to get that popsicle or you're going to get the dollar bill in an envelope."

LEARNING SELF-AWARENESS

An important dimension of EQ is self-awareness. For example, my day can be packed with clients. But if I don't take time to have a snack and to eat lunch, I get low blood sugar and start to feel so tired I can barely keep my eyes open. When that happens because I'm not paying attention to my own needs, I'm not serving my clients very well either. In my experience, lack of self-awareness about eating is common but often overlooked and can cause problems. I've had many clients come to me for coaching because their bosses say they had anger issues. After sitting with the client for a while, I would think, *Gosh, it's hard for me to believe that this guy has anger issues. It's just not coming out.* When that happens, I make sure to ask the clients, as part of the general "getting-to-know-you" type questions, to tell me about their morning routine before they leave the house for work. Often I find they don't eat breakfast and don't get around to lunch until 1 p.m. if they eat lunch at all. When they're in a meeting at 11 a.m., they get irritable and angry just because they're so low on fuel that they can't hold anything in, particularly if they have feelings of displeasure when someone is speaking.

The real issue with these clients is that their self-awareness is low—they don't really have anger issues. I help them raise their EQ in this area by using techniques like documenting what time they eat, documenting what time their meetings were, documenting how they felt during the meeting. We discover the links that way. Maybe it's that they didn't eat, or they didn't get enough sleep so they had five cups of coffee. That got them so amped up that anything was going to agitate them.

When someone isn't self-aware, a small change can have a big impact. That's where I can help. For my client who supposedly had anger issues, the solution was simply to make sure he took those extra 15 minutes in the morning to eat a reasonable breakfast.

LEARNING LEADERSHIP

Some people just naturally take control. They walk into a room and suddenly everybody turns toward them and wants to hear what they have to say. Those people, well, possibly they were born natural leaders. Not everybody has that natural quality, and yet there are many people who can be good leaders. As long as they have high emotional intelligence skills or are willing to improve their lower categories, they can be taught how to be a good leader.

Both EQ and leadership can be taught, just like a kid can be taught how to ride a bike or tie her shoes. People can be taught how to be more empathetic; people can be taught to self-regulate more effectively. There are tools that they can learn to use to help them regain control quickly if they get angry or upset.

Of course, learning to ride a bike does involve falling off from time to time. It takes practice to ride a bike easily, without thinking about it, and even then you might crash sometimes if you aren't paying attention. Learning to lead by improving your emotional intelligence is much the same. It's not painless, and it's not effortless, but it's worth it. Just as riding a bike is fun and gives you a great sense of feeling in control, better EQ lets you get more out of your work and your life. Once you learn to ride a bike, you never forget. Also, once you learn, it's almost impossible to fall off accidentally. Your body memory takes over, as does emotional intelligence memory, I suspect. Your body simply knows how to keep you on an even keel. It's the same with EQ skills. Once you learn them and incorporate them into your life, you have them for good.

Some people have the innate ability to lead. Those who don't, but have a passion to achieve something, can certainly learn skills and exhibit qualities that make them effective leaders.

So what are the qualities of an effective leader?

Vision

Motivating a group of people can be complicated. Sharing a vision of what needs to be accomplished is necessary. Without vision, there is no clear purpose. And without purpose, you cannot set appropriate goals or develop strategies for reaching them. Develop a brief description of the vision, and make sure everyone understands and is on board with it at the outset.

Passion

What is truly meaningful to you? What are you determined to accomplish? When you can answer these questions, you will find self-motivation. For example, a colleague was 100 percent sure she wanted to attend Florida State University and major in psychology. Her parents couldn't afford to pay for the tuition, but the strong desire deep inside of her to get to FSU was all the motivation she needed. Nothing was going to stop her. She spent many hours—long before the Internet—researching scholarships and student loans so she could follow her passion. The saying "Where there's a will, there's a way" is so true! She had to work part-time and pay off student loans—but she valued the education she received and the whole experience all the more because her passion got her there.

Honesty

Be a role model for the type of behavior and communication that you expect from others on your team. Integrity is essential. People will lose respect for you if you are perceived as dishonest or if your intentions are selfish and not in the best interest of the group. Some may even lie or withhold information from you to get things done. You don't want to be an obstacle to your team. Look at your motivation, and if you haven't been honest, then get honest and get the team back on track.

Delegation

Trust others to complete tasks. The more work you take on, the more likely it is that the quality of your work will suffer. Identify the strengths of teams and individuals and try to give them work they will most likely enjoy doing. This will make them feel trusted and motivate them to be successful in the task at hand. Delegation done right will improve the overall quality of work and increase personal satisfaction in your people.

Communication

Communicate your requests clearly and explicitly. Don't assume that people know what you're talking about or that they come from your same experiences. If you don't clearly communicate your instructions or the desired result, others may misinterpret your wishes. This could lead to frustration and tension on both sides. Be prepared to communicate your dissatisfaction when required. A big mistake that many leaders make is to avoid conflict or confrontations. Anticipate where problems might occur and reflect on how you may need to have hard conversations with difficult or confrontational people. Encourage people to have open yet respectful conversations with you and with one another by modeling and supporting open communication.

Laughter

Keeping your sense of humor and staying positive when things go wrong can be very powerful. Mistakes keep us human, and we can even learn from them. Technology can be unreliable at times. Stuff just happens. It's life. When your team sees that their leader can laugh things off, see the positive in a negative situation, and keep a positive temper about them, they are more likely to model the same behavior. That allows the group to continue to move forward without dwelling on mistakes or feeling shame.

Confidence

Sometimes, things don't go as planned. If the leader loses confidence, then the team will follow. The leader's job is to step up to the plate and show the others that you are confident they will do better next time. Let them know that you have confidence and that all is not doom and gloom. Show them that your feet are planted firmly and you are ready to move forward successfully.

Commitment

Practice what you preach. If you expect a clean environment, set the standards for others by showing you are willing to pick up trash and dispose of it properly when you see it. If you expect positive energy, exude positive energy. If you expect detail in their work, show your work in detail. If you want people to do more than is expected, you must be committed to going above and beyond yourself. Be willing to give recognition and to celebrate their hard work and efforts. Recognition and praise go a long way.

Positivity

Create positive energy in your group or organization that will motivate, rejuvenate, and inspire. Bring their favorite treats, celebrate birthdays, give out certificates of accomplishment, or recognize individuals in emails or group meetings. It is amazing what people will do for you when there is positive energy in the group. People will want to do things for you and go the extra mile when needed!

Creativity

Leaders sometimes get caught in sticky situations. They have to make decisions that no one else wants to make. Effective leaders can think outside of the box. Show your team that you have confidence and respect for them by including them in the decision-making process. They will feel valued when you solicit their opinions. Be careful not to make decisions too quickly. Weigh pros and cons after you have considered the input of others.

Intuition

When you find yourself in a situation where you're not sure what to do, trust your instincts. Consider past experiences. Reflect on what your mentor might do. Better yet, contact your mentor for support. If you don't trust yourself to make decisions for the group, then they will lose confidence in you as well. Make a decision and stick to it. Going back and forth will create doubt in people's minds and reduce your effectiveness as a leader.

Inspiration

Effective leaders have the ability to inspire a group of individuals to share a common vision or goal. Individuals and groups understand their role and take ownership of the work they do. The final outcome is successful because all involved have given it their best.

I believe that anyone with a clear vision and the passion to bring that vision to life has the motivation to become a successful leader! That's why I wrote this book. Start practicing the skills you'll learn here, and watch the impact you have on people.

WHAT TYPE OF LEADER ARE YOU?

A leader is best described as a person who invests in others, empowers them to excel, and challenges them to exceed their best. How does your leadership style influence others? Are you quick to point out weaknesses? How has that worked for you? Let's face it—most people already know their weaknesses because they've been pointed out to them in the past, and they have suffered setbacks because of them. Instead of dwelling on the negatives, a good leader will give people the triple-A treatment: attention, affirmation, and appreciation.

Attention

The next time you're with someone, give your undivided attention through eye contact and reflective listening. Then ask a question based on what you've just heard. When someone knows you have truly heard, you have made a real connection and paved the way for a positive relationship. I'll give some practical advice for being a better listener in chapter 9.

Affirmation

Affirming someone is a gift to the giver and receiver. We can affirm others just by supporting them or even validating them. When an employee has a new idea, even if it's questionable, congratulating the employee for thinking outside the box is a way of affirming. Affirmation is an easy gift to give that can yield wonderful results! Today, think of one way that you can affirm the people in your life who count on you to mentor, guide, and lead them. One way could be as simple as agreeing with a new idea someone suggests, even if you, as the leader, aren't quite sure about it. You never know—down the road it might turn out to be a winner.

Appreciation

Show your appreciation for someone through words or actions, and you will be amazed at the response. Psychologist Henry H. Goddard conducted a study on children and their energy levels using an instrument called the "ergograph." He discovered when a tired child was given a word of encouragement or appreciation, the ergograph showed an upward surge of energy in the child. When they were criticized or discouraged, the ergograph showed their physical energy take a sudden nosedive. What kind of energy are you creating for your staff? Are you encouraging them and being an energy carrier, or are you draining their energy?

QUALITIES OF A GOOD LEADER

Through years of working and coaching I've learned what makes good leaders and then what can make a good leader *great*! And high EQ is something all great leaders have in common. The following qualities should be in place to start:

L | A good leader is a good *Listener.* This can't be stressed enough. Everyone enjoys being around a good listener and feels very special to be listened to intently … especially by a person who is important to them or their career.

E | A good leader exhibits *Excellence* in the field or at least the profession. This excellence can be from education, practical experience, or trained experience.

A | A good *Attitude* can become the "difference maker" in your life, opening doors and helping you and those around you to overcome great obstacles. People thrive on being around positivity and working for leaders with a positive attitude.

D | A good leader offers *Direction.* Connect with those you lead, and give them the inspiration, insight, and direction they need. Good leaders also exhibit *Discernment,* the ability to find the root of the matter, relying on intuition as well as rational thought. Discernment is an indispensable quality for any leader who desires to maximize effectiveness.

E | A good leader exhibits *Excellence* by always doing his best and expecting the best of others. A good leader is also an *Enlarger,* someone who can always see beyond today and works to become better, not only because it benefits them personally but also because it helps them to help others.

R | A good leader takes *Responsibility.* A leader can delegate anything, except responsibility! Leaders face whatever life and business throw their way and give it their best. A good leader takes responsibility for anything that goes wrong, even when it's the fault of someone else and never leaves you high and dry to take the heat.

Look inside yourself, and identify which qualities you exemplify and which you need to work on. Becoming a great leader is an ongoing process that depends a lot on your EQ. If you're willing to improve your EQ skills, you can automatically improve your ability to lead.

Case Study:
Improving Self-Awareness

A few years ago, I started coaching Michael S. He was a middle manager in a very large corporation who felt stuck and unhappy in his job. He wanted to move up, but he never seemed to be chosen for leadership roles.

When we started exploring his emotional intelligence, we discovered that his overall self-awareness was very low. Over the next eight months, we focused on improving his leadership traits. Through coaching, he was able to become a better listener, improve his attitude, give better direction to his employees, and take responsibility for himself and his team.

We focused on some very specific issues. Michael had a tendency toward angry outbursts, meaning he had a problem with self-regulation. But because he was also low in self-awareness, he never realized that his angry outbursts really upset everyone around him and made a bad impression on the people above.

To help him become more self-aware, I had Michael keep a little notebook in his pocket so he could write down the time whenever he felt agitated or yelled at someone. When we looked at his "schedule," we saw that his anger was always when he had skipped breakfast and hadn't eaten anything for several hours— usually in the late morning. We also found a connection between staying up late playing video games and yelling at people the next day. Low blood sugar and sleep deprivation were clearly playing a role here.

We decided Michael would eliminate the late-night video games. I introduced him to books I knew he would enjoy reading and got him to go on a better sleep schedule. I literally said, "Okay, at 10, read your book for 30 minutes or so, put it down, and go to bed." Suddenly, he was less agitated and less angry. His significant other said he was a lot less moody—something he was able to accomplish simply by quitting the video games, replacing that activity with a pleasant read, and going to bed at a reasonable hour.

Because Michael was so unaware of his emotions or the way he felt, period, I would have him set timers at six different times during the day. When the timer went off, he was to document how he felt in his notebook. The goal was to bring him in tune with how he felt, because he had no idea. When we reviewed his emotional diary, we were able to pinpoint how he let his emotional responses to others overwhelm him. Just by seeing this, Michael became much more aware of his reactions and was better able to regulate his emotions.

Michael came to me because he thought he hated his job. In fact, he just didn't like himself and his life. Because of my training in intrinsic coaching, I was able to help him get to the core issue. The core question for

Michael was, "What do you want?" I would ask him and ask him, and we spent a long time getting to it.

He would say, "I want a new job. I want my girlfriend to act right. I want this, I want this, and I want this." And then finally he said, "You know what? I really just want to feel better." Instead of wanting things outside him to change, we finally got to his intrinsic issue—"I just want to feel better." From there, we were able to really work through his EQ issues and get him to be much more self-aware and self-regulated.

Michael was able to move from a work situation that made him unhappy and where he was on the verge of being fired to finally getting promoted. He's still with the same corporation, but now he makes a lot more money, has more responsibility, and is a lot happier.

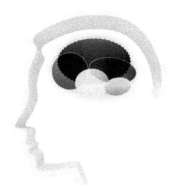

CHAPTER 2

The Value of EQ

E motional intelligence is the ability to sense, understand, and effectively apply the power and acumen of emotions to facilitate high levels of collaboration and productivity. Emotional intelligence is crucial for successful leadership.

EQ has four realms: perceiving emotions, understanding emotions, using emotions, and managing emotions. Leaders who have these qualities far, far exceed other leaders. It's why they're star performers.

WHY EQ MATTERS TO INDIVIDUALS

EQ matters to you as an individual in the workplace, because the bottom line is that the employees and the individuals within a company are like the shareholders of that company. They literally control the destiny of the company. The leader is important, but each individual is also hugely important. Collectively, individuals who use their emotions well will make the workplace more harmonious and productive for everyone. As an individual, you'll enjoy your work more. You will have better work performance and better physical health. You'll be more in tune with yourself and know how to make yourself feel better—for example, by going to bed early because you didn't sleep well the night before.

With a better work/life balance, people realize "family is just as important as my job," and they'll go home at 5 p.m. and take care of their kids. Maybe they'll turn on the computer for 30 minutes that night and get some additional work done, but they're not going to dwell on spending three hours at the computer at night because they didn't finish up. They generally have better mental health because they're more self-aware. They have better relationships because they're easier to be around.

The bottom line is that people don't care how much you know if knowledge is all you have to offer. They notice how much you care about them. If a leader or an employee cares about those around them, people want to be around them more and are more willing to work hard to please them. People with higher EQ have a way of letting others do things their own way. When someone suggests doing something differently, a high EQ leader says, "That's a good idea," and lets the person try it. Because people with high EQ are just more agreeable, they don't create conflict and controversy. Working with them leads to a feeling of collaboration rather than of manipulation.

People with higher EQ generally feel more peace in their lives. I know for myself that when I'm self-aware and when I'm regulating my tongue, I'm kind to others and I have a team approach to everybody around me. I'm much more pleasant to be around, so my life runs more smoothly, and that, in turn, makes it easier to be on a team with me.

WHY EQ MATTERS FOR COMPANIES

EQ starts at the top. If the leaders have high EQ and feel secure in themselves, they'll generally hire people who are similar. Leaders tend to hire people who are like them. A leader with high EQ will be more drawn to people who also have a high EQ—and are less apt to attract people who don't.

When company leaders, managers, and employees have high EQ, productivity soars. When people are self-aware, they're happier, more peaceful, and more willing to work collaboratively with each other.

MORE SALES AND BETTER SERVICE

To increase sales and attain better service ratings, leaders with high EQ know the importance of engaging in active listening, which is a technique that I train all of my leaders to do (I'll talk more about it in chapter 9). This applies not only to potential and current clients but to employees. When you actively listen to your employees, you will learn from them and they will feel enlarged by your doing so. Listening also enhances your staff's thinking about how to get the job done.

When it comes to customer service, EQ studies have shown that when salespeople and customer service agents go through EQ assessments and training, they develop more accounts, they have higher sales, they deliver stronger customer service, and they experience greater customer retention than those who have not had any EQ training. Their earning potential jumps, as the story of Kim S. will show at the end of this chapter.

BETTER RETENTION WITH EQ

A manager with high EQ is more likely to retain employees and avoid expensive, disruptive turnover. Why? Because people are going to be more satisfied. There's going to be more collaboration. People will be heard. Their ideas are going to be listened to. They're going to enjoy the workplace more—a whole lot more. There will be less calling in sick and less ducking out at 4:40.

An employee with high EQ is more likely to find satisfaction in his or her work and get along with the other workers better. But because a worker with high EQ is also a more desirable employee who could easily go elsewhere, he expects high EQ from a manager. He wants a workplace where he feels valued and will look for one someplace else if he does not. When high EQ employees come together with high EQ leaders, companies can really thrive.

CONFLICT RESOLUTION

When a leader has high EQ, dealing with difficult people and conflict resolution become much easier. Even the best performer is sometimes going to have a difficult day. Someone who's high in EQ will know how to acknowledge the conflict, such as by saying, "I'm feeling some tension here. Let's talk about what's going on." Without EQ, the reaction is more likely to be, "I don't know what's going on here but stop it."

A good leader is respectful. I think if you disagree with someone respectfully, as opposed to just cutting them off, they're a lot more likely to respect your decision and not try to undermine it. They may not like it, but they'll go along with it.

I spend a lot of time coaching managers on how to use EQ to avoid conflict and then to resolve it when it does arise. No workplace is ever conflict free, but when EQ is in place, the problems tend to be less severe and more easily resolved.

A book I often recommend to my clients is *Developing the Leader Within You,* by leadership expert John C. Maxwell. It's inspirational and easy to read, even funny in a lot of places. I often ask my clients to just read a single page a day. Among other things, Maxwell is an expert in conflict resolution. His advice comes down to what he calls The 10 Commandments of Confrontation. When I work with managers who want to improve their leadership skills, I use the commandments as our starting point.

• •

Maxwell's 10 Commandments of Confrontation

1. Do it privately, not publicly.

2. Do it as soon as possible.

3. Focus on one issue at a time.

4. Once you've made a point, don't keep repeating it.

5. Deal only with actions the person can change. If you ask the person to do something he or she is unable to do, frustration builds in your relationship.

6. Avoid sarcasm.

7. Avoid words like "always" and "never."

8. Present criticisms as suggestions or questions, if possible.

9. Don't apologize for the confrontational meeting. Doing so detracts from it and may indicate you are not sure you had the right to say what you did.

10. Don't forget the compliments. Use the sandwich method: Compliment—Confront—Compliment.

. . . .

To Maxwell's commandments, I add my own commandment 11: "Don't ask someone why."

Avoid asking someone "Why did you screw up that report?" "Why did you do that?" "Why did you show up late?" "Why did you confront that employee?" As soon as you say "why" to someone, it's like saying "why" to a teenager. It's the most toxic word in the vocabulary, I think. When you say it, they're going to tune you out. That applies to personal relationships as well as the workplace. I demonstrate this to my clients with a simple exercise. I have the client lean back in the chair, close his eyes, and relax. Then I say to him, "Why did you do that?" Invariably, his eyes snap open, he sits up suddenly, and he gets tense. That's not the way to begin a productive discussion.

Case Study:
More Sales through Better EQ

One of my clients, Kim S., was a productive sales rep for a big national company. She came to me because she was losing some sales and didn't know why. Kim is very empathetic, but her listening skills—an aspect of self-awareness—were lacking. She would get so excited toward the close of the sale that she would start talking and talking and talking and talking. There were a couple of times when she talked herself out of a sale. She told me, "Sometimes the client has the paperwork, and we're just chatting while he fills it out. I'd be asking him about his kids and this and this and this." Because she wasn't self-aware of how she affected other people, she didn't realize that she was distracting, and even annoying, the client at a crucial moment.

I worked with Kim on ways to close the deal and then close her mouth. We came up with a visual image of her literally pretending that she was putting masking tape on her mouth and she was not to say another word. It took some practice, but Kim made it work and saw her sales numbers go up.

By improving her EQ, Kim was a happier, more confident person and a more productive sales rep. Her income went up $40,000 because she was closing more sales.

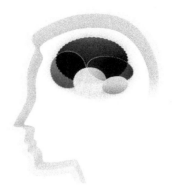

CHAPTER 3

Measuring Emotional Intelligence

Exactly how much emotional intelligence do you have? In what areas are you strongest? EQ can be measured in many ways, and there are a variety of validated assessment tools to choose from. One of the assessment tools I'll discuss later looks at behaviors, motivators, and competencies and includes an EQ component. But all assessment tools that measure EQ focus on these five dimensions:

- Self-awareness
- Self-regulation
- Motivation
- Empathy
- Social skills

Let's take them one at a time.

SELF-AWARENESS

Self-awareness is the ability to recognize and understand your moods, emotions, and drives, as well as their effect on others. Self-awareness is knowing how you're feeling and why you're feeling that way. It's knowing your personal strengths and limits and having an accurate sense of your self-worth and capabilities.

People who are high in self-awareness know how they're feeling. For example, if they are usually very neat and orderly and see that their desks or surroundings are messy, they know they won't be able to think creatively that day because of the mess. Or maybe they're in a bad mood because someone cut them off in traffic or they spilled coffee on the rug that morning. Someone with low EQ might not even realize why the bad mood is there. Someone with high EQ would know "Okay, well that happened. I just need to get over myself, clean the rug, and move on."

Being high in self-awareness means being sensitive to your own moods and how your body feels. If you know you have a tendency toward depression or anxiety, for instance, being self-aware helps you to monitor your mood. If you're aware that you're feeling a bit depressed that day, then you'll be especially careful when evaluating something that comes up at the office. Maybe hormonal or other physical changes are a factor. Is the office issue that big of a problem, or is your mood making it seem so? If you're self-aware, you'll know the difference and act accordingly.

Another important aspect of self-awareness is knowing your own strengths and limits. I coach the president of a large company. He's a great visionary, but he's not good at details. He was starting to get overwhelmed by his work. We came to the conclusion that he needed to hire an executive assistant who was good in all the areas he was not. He found exactly the right woman to help him handle all the day-to-day details. He still had a problem, however, with wanting to help every employee who came to him with a problem. He wasn't good at screening out those who could easily be helped by his executive assistant instead of by him. He knew this wasn't a strong area for him—and he didn't want to be strong in it. We came up with a solution. He would listen to each person for five minutes, then decide who to pass on to his assistant. By giving each employee five minutes, which even he could do, he eliminated all that stress for himself.

Another important category of self-awareness is having a sense of your self-worth and capability. We have to realize our capabilities. We need to know what we're good at, what we like to do, and when to hand things over to someone else. I personally love marketing, but to do everything I need to do to market successfully is just too time-consuming and takes me away from my coaching. I found someone who can do it twice as fast and twice as cleverly. I'm happy to pay her to do it.

SELF-REGULATION

Self-regulation is the ability to control or redirect disruptive impulses and moods and the propensity to suspend judgment and think before acting. For example, a person with good self-regulation will keep disruptive emotions and impulses in check. I had a client once who was at a board meeting for her company. She was talking to a board member and managed to trip and spill coffee all over the other woman. The woman on the receiving end of the coffee clearly had high EQ. Rather than getting annoyed, she started laughing.

She told my client, "The best part about this is that not only do I not drink coffee, I hate even the smell of coffee." Despite that, she handled it beautifully. She didn't get angry with my client—she just went into the ladies room and got cleaned up. I would say she's pretty high in self-regulation. Nobody would have blamed her for being annoyed, but she chose to treat the incident with humor instead.

Self-regulation means maintaining standards of honesty and integrity. When people in the corporation see the leader as being honest and always doing the right thing no matter what, even when it's not the easiest thing, it really gives everybody a sense of warmth and community. It takes a person with high self-regulation to be able to do that.

Self-regulation also means taking responsibility for personal performance. Leaders with high EQ are absolutely going to take responsibility not only for their own actions but also take responsibility for the team. They'll take one for the team if they have to. Even if the team does something wrong, they'll say, "Well that was under my jurisdiction, and I'm to blame."

Someone with high self-regulation is also flexible in handling change. Let's say a key person decides to go to work for a competitor. Inside, a leader may feel very stressed about that, but externally, they're going to handle it very diplomatically and be happy for the departing employee and be very flexible with what it can do for the company. Leadership means not taking it personally.

High self-regulation means that a leader is comfortable with new ideas, new approaches, and new information. When an employee brings up an idea that is just absurd, they have enough self-regulation to say, "You know, that might be a possibility. We'll have to look further into that," as opposed to saying, "You've got to be kidding me." New ideas that sound crazy at first may end up being really valuable.

MOTIVATION

Motivation is a passion to work for reasons that rise above money or status. It's a propensity to pursue goals with energy and persistence by striving to meet or exceed a standard of excellence.

Someone with high motivation might have a plan of action that's already good enough, but he'll continue to strive to make it even better or perfect it. That's even if it means working a few extra hours or researching another topic that might make it even better or make it stand out to the boss or to the client.

A person with high motivation is going to always make sure, regardless of what their own beliefs are, that they're reaching the goals and striving to make the group look good and the company look good. Highly motivated leaders align with the goals of a group or organization, even if they don't necessarily believe that it's what they would do if they were in charge. When you're planning something in the military, you make your best case for what you want to do. When the people above you disagree, you don't get to quit. Instead, you salute and march.

Someone with high motivation is always ready to act on opportunities. They're always ready to be the first to volunteer to take on something new. Even if their plate is full, highly motivated people are always the first to say, "I'll help with that community project," or "I'll step in," when somebody else is ill or out working on another project.

Motivation leads to persistence in pursuing goals, despite obstacles and setbacks. If there's a barrier to the plan or the goal, they will constantly look for ways to go under it, around it, or over it. I have a client who owns several franchises. He's looking to add six more, but he keeps hitting roadblocks and setbacks with his potential investors. At one point, he said to me, "Maybe it's just not meant for me to do this."

I replied, "Absolutely not. You'll find the people you need."

He said, "Well, I'm going to keep doing it, but it's hard."

I told him, "Just remember, with every no you get, you're closer to a yes." He wrote that on his hand and left my office, ready to start in with more phone calls to potential investors. Even highly motivated people can get discouraged, but this client was so motivated that all it took was writing a slogan on his hand to get him fired up again.

EMPATHY

Empathy is the ability to understand the emotional makeup of other people. Those with high empathy are skilled at sensing other's feelings and perspectives and taking an active interest in their concerns. Someone who's high in empathy can be working away and hear someone sigh two cubicles away. They'll literally get up and go try to help that person, just because they know that if they can help someone, the whole environment's going to be better. They sense it because they are high in empathy.

Someone high in empathy can tell what other people need and want. They know how to bolster others and support them. A boss high in empathy would know when an employee is ready for a promotion, for example. But if the employee knows there is no position available for her, she might leave the company rather than wait for something to open up. Before she starts looking around, an empathetic boss would sit down and talk with her, explain the long-term plan, and promise that the next promotion slot will be hers, probably in a few months. That promise and timeline will motivate and retain a valuable employee.

Empathy allows a leader to anticipate issues by recognizing and meeting the needs of others. Let's say that the promotion opportunity promised to the employee from the example above doesn't come through after a few months. A good leader recognizes that this will be a problem and sits down with the employee to explain the situation honestly. He might say, "The position isn't going to be available when I thought, but corporate is working on it, and it will be available in the next month." This empathetic anticipation defuses the situation and keeps the employee from being disgruntled.

Empathy is also helpful for cultivating opportunities among the employees. Empathetic leaders generally tend to surround themselves with a variety of people with different skill sets and different mindsets. They'll cultivate each one and also help them develop other skills that maybe they don't have by teaming them up with their fellow employees who do. I have a client who is really good at this. He'll acknowledge one employee for his strength in one particular area and then partner him on a project with someone who's not strong in that area but is strong in something else. When they work together, they learn from each other. They both get better at their jobs. This intuitive understanding of your employees allows you to put together the best possible team.

SOCIAL SKILLS

Social skills are proficiency in managing relationships and building networks. Those with good social skills are particularly suited for wielding effective tactics for persuasion—one of the qualities necessary for a good salesperson. In any leadership role, being able to be persuasive is crucial for getting everyone on board with your decisions.

People with good social skills are good at listening openly and sending convincing messages. The best way to do this is through active listening. For example, let's say it's time to decide between two plans. A leader listens to his people and says, "What I hear you saying is we should implement Plan B. You don't believe in Plan A, and I agree." By sending that convincing message of "I agree," the whole team agrees.

Good social skills are also valuable for negotiating and resolving disagreements. This goes back to being able to acknowledge that there's a problem right away and not ignoring it. A leader with good social skills doesn't talk down to anyone and definitely doesn't ask "Why?" when solving a disagreement.

A leader with good social skills inspires and guides individuals and groups by enlarging them. What I mean by that is asking them to tell you what they feel about a particular topic. By doing so, they get insight into the issue and are inspired to use their own creativity to solve it. Everyone has the knowledge; they need the inspiration and guidance of a good leader to be sure they're right.

People high in social skills aren't afraid of change. They actually initiate and embrace change, because they know it will invite more success.

Leaders with good social skills are good at nurturing relationships and building bonds. They take the time to learn about the people they work with, about what's going on in their personal lives, learning what their hobbies are, learning what their likes and dislikes are. A leader will take the trouble to find out what employees' favorite types of cake are so that when they have a birthday, their favorite cake is served.

Because they have high social skills, they're great at working with others toward shared goals. They love being a part of the team. They're not an "I," they live in the "we." They love the group dynamic. They establish cohesiveness within the group as well as keeping conflicts at a minimum. They create group synergy and get everyone pursuing collective goals.

Our emotions have a psychological effect on us before we even realize it. This dates back to our human survival instincts of fight or flight. This natural instinct doesn't necessarily serve us well when it comes to making decisions in our personal and professional lives. But by reviewing the above aspects of what makes someone have high EQ, you can determine what comes most naturally to you and what areas need more development. You may be strong in one area and lacking in another. By reviewing each aspect with this in mind, you have a solid base for further development.

TOOLS FOR MEASURING EQ

We can measure EQ in a lot of ways—many companies offer validated assessment tools. In general, EQ is measured using questionnaires that ask somewhere between 150 and 200 personality-based questions. There aren't any right or wrong answers on an EQ assessment.

I like to use an excellent online assessment tool from a company called TTI SUCCESS INSIGHTS, which looks at three sciences: behaviors, motivators, and competencies. The results of the TriMetrix assessments used by TTI have been studied and validated—they're quite accurate. Depending on what the company or client wants, we can do the full TriMetrix assessment, which includes an EQ component, or we can do a shorter version that looks primarily at personality and behavior using DISC (I'll explain that in the next section).

Assessments (I don't like to call them tests—it turns a lot of people off) are valuable because they help individuals understand themselves better. They give awareness of what makes you tick. When assessments are done with a team, it helps all the team members understand themselves better and also understand each other better.

One example of this really stands out in my mind. Georgia, the executive director of a corporate client, contacted me after hearing me give a presentation. She said, "I'd really like to hire you to work with Cathy, one of my managers. She's the most trustworthy, loyal, dedicated employee I've ever had, but she's not that productive. My problem is that I dread talking to her. When I go in to ask her a question, she goes off on a tangent and I don't even know what she's talking about. She gets her team so confused that they don't have any respect for her, and they don't get things done. I want to hold on to her, but she needs some help."

Because I've done this a lot, I thought I knew what was going on: two different communications styles were clashing. I went to company headquarters and had both Georgia and Cathy take a basic TriMetrix assessment. Then I sat down with each of them individually, behind closed doors, and went through the assessments with them so that they could understand themselves better.

After reviewing Georgia's individual results, I went back to the assessment and said, "Now look at this one page and tell me what qualities Cathy possesses." After she told me, I said, "The assessment tells you right here how to communicate with someone like her. And because you two are so totally different, what does it tell you?" She realized that based on the assessment, she needed to bond with Cathy whenever she needed to approach her.

Only after that could she then say, "Tell me what's going on."

The executive director wasn't happy with this. She said, "I have to be very patient, because she's going to be very descriptive? I hate communicating that way!"

I pointed out, "That's just the way Cathy communicates. As the executive director, you have to learn how to communicate with her, but I can also teach Cathy how to communicate better with you."

I then took Cathy through the same exercise. We looked at her assessment, and I said, "Cathy, find the words that describe your boss here." She found the description of her boss: demanding, strong-willed, direct, futuristic thinker, and so on—the total opposite of Cathy.

I asked her what the assessment told her about communicating with Georgia. Cathy said, "Don't worry about bonding, get straight to the point, give her some facts, and don't give her any fluff."

I said, "So what do you see wrong here?"

She said, "I think I've been giving her too much information, and she can't handle it. But when she comes in I feel threatened."

When I asked her what felt threatening, she said, "Georgia walks in, and she immediately taps my desk and says, 'So tell me what's going on.' I feel like I'm being attacked." Was she? Not really—that was just the way Georgia communicated, by getting straight to the point.

Next, I brought them both to the conference room together and showed them the other one's assessment (with their permission, of course). They both just broke down in tears. Cathy said to Georgia, "We've been working together all these years … I never understood why you were so agitated with me."

And Georgia responded, "I wasn't agitated with you, I just didn't understand," and they went back and forth. I didn't ask either one to change her communication style. All I did was help them understand each other better.

After working more with me on confidence, how to approach her team, and various other things uncovered by her TriMetrix assessment (which included the EQ component), Cathy continued to be a trustworthy, dedicated employee—but now she was also productive. A win-win all the way around!

THE TRIMETRIX DISC ASSESSMENT TOOL

One of the most widely used and accurate assessment tools for evaluating personality and behavior as part of emotional intelligence is the DISC. The DISC tool measures behavior in four areas:

D: DOMINANCE

I : INFLUENCING

S: STEADINESS

C: COMPLIANCE

The traits are rated on a scale of 1 to 100. The results can be revealing. For example, on compliance, I'm a 7—very low. That means that working in an organization where there are a lot of rules is beyond what I can do. I'm not a good fit for working in a bank or a big insurance company; I would just go nuts, stressed because there'd be so many rules. On the other hand, I'm a top performer in my Business Network International (BNI) group—in fact, my peers voted me Member of the Year in 2014. I have a lot of rules to follow there—four one-on-one meetings a month, bringing a visitor once a month, continuing education requirements, and more. I follow those rules 100 percent. Why? Not because I'm good at it or like it, but because I'm motivated: It's my reputation. But I also enjoy it because I rank very high on the influencing scale. I love to refer and link up people. It's fun for me.

The DISC assessment is a sort of questionnaire. It takes about an hour to complete. Based on your answers, the tool determines your percentage in each category. In addition to the number, the tool gives word descriptors for each category. For example, somebody who's high in the dominance category would be assertive, ambitious, driven, strong-willed, and decisive. Somebody who's high in influencing is more enthusiastic, sociable, charming, and persuasive. Somebody who's high in steadiness is patient, stable, predictable, consistent, a good listener. Someone who's high in compliance is detailed, meticulous, systematic, and neat.

The results of the DISC are valuable for providing insight into the behavior of an individual. The DISC doesn't look at emotional intelligence or what motivates someone, however. For that, we use an additional motivator's component. The motivators assessment looks at six motivators:

1. Theoretical—hypothetical, academic, notional, conjectural, abstract; the desire to learn more, passion for knowledge

2. Utilitarian—useful, practical, serviceable, no-frills, down-to-earth, effective; a passion for the future or a passion for the exchange of money or the exchange of information
3. Aesthetic—drawn to beauty with a passion
4. Social—communal, societal, public, shared, collective, group; a passion for other people
5. Traditional—customary, conventional, usual, established, fixed, long-established, time-honored, habitual, accepted; a preference for being within a strong, efficient system
6. Individualistic—unusual, distinctive, original, characteristic, personal, peculiar, unique; someone strong and individualistic who likes being in the spotlight

Individualism is the most flexible of all motivators. We often see this trait in CEOs, visionaries, and politicians—people who are good at the big picture.

What's so helpful about understanding someone's motivators is that you can work with them as individuals. Let's say you have someone on your team and you want to give her a raise, but it's just not in the budget. You know from her EQ assessment, however, that she's more the aesthetic type. She doesn't care that much about money as a motivation for working. So you offer to move her to an office with a nicer view. Or maybe you're in the same situation with a good employee who's more the theoretical type. You can offer to send him for additional training. In both cases, you've made the employees happy, motivated them, kept them from moving to another company, and stayed within your budget.

When we look at the motivators, we usually see that people have two high categories, which are their primary motivators—the things that will always get their attention. The next two depend largely on the situation for motivation—sometimes these motivators matter but not always. The remaining two are of little importance to the person and don't really motivate at all.

The DISC assessment also looks at competencies such as goal orientation, personal effectiveness, self-confidence, resilience, persuasion, written communication, flexibility, and others. By looking at how you rate on the various competencies, you get a competency hierarchy that tells you where your strengths and weaknesses lie.

WHY USE THE DISC?

When I have one of my clients take a DISC assessment, our goal is to find clarity. What characteristics are strong, what are weak? How do your competencies fit with what your job requires?

Often a client comes to me convinced that he or she needs a new job because they're unhappy in the current situation. When we talk, I'm not always convinced that changing jobs is the answer. To find out more, I ask the client where he thinks his talents lie. We make a list, and then I have him do the DISC assessment. When we discuss the results, I'm able to show typical behaviors and explain what the natural behaviors are and what the adapted behaviors are. If their behaviors aren't changing much, they're pretty much in line with what they see as their talents.

What the DISC often tells us is that people don't really need to change jobs. Instead, they need to discuss the other issues in their motivation and competencies. The DISC makes those very apparent. For example, if a client is high in steadiness and compliance, a sales career is probably not a good fit for them. Additionally, this person wouldn't be a good entrepreneur because, generally, entrepreneurs need at least a moderate level of dominance in their natural behaviors. Someone high in influencing and dominance would make a good salesperson and entrepreneur or team leader. One combination that is difficult for people is the one who is high in dominance and compliance. The reason is that the high dominant is a take-charge decision-maker, but the compliance can slow down the decision-making process by making sure every rule is being followed, while high dominance isn't usually concerned with the black-and-white rules. This can cause an internal conflict in the high dominant and high compliant leader. There are many more combinations that can be explained, but this is a small sample of some.

Never was this clearer to me than with one of my clients, Matt O. Matt has a thriving body shop business servicing high-end cars. The shop does really well. He's dying to open second and third locations. In our coaching sessions, we talked about this. I kept saying, "I really don't think you should do that." When he asked why, I said, "You know I'm not about stopping anybody from success, but I feel like it is going to create so much stress for you. You like being able to see your whole work environment in one glance, you like knowing what's going on everywhere, you like a steady pace, and you like for your day to be consistent."

Well, he agreed with me, but he was also arguing with me. So I said, "You've been putting off taking the assessment for a year and a half. Let's do it, and you'll see."

He argued and argued and argued but finally took it. The day we were scheduled to discuss the results, he came in and said, "Before we go through this I have to tell you what I just did. I just put a lot of money down on land for our second location."

And I said, "Oh, my God. Are you going to be able to get that money back?"

He said, "Why do you keep asking that?"

I said, "Let's go through your assessment, and then you tell me what you think you should do." When we went through his results, sure enough he was high in steadiness, he didn't like a change in his pace, he didn't like being in many places during the day, he liked his own little environment, and he liked it to be consistent. The assessment proved that he wouldn't be happy with two locations and trying to know what was going on in both places. He picked up the phone and canceled the bid right in my office.

The assessment helped Matt get some insight into his own thinking. When he saw it in black-and-white, he was convinced. I knew he would be. From the start, I could tell that Matt would be very high in the steadiness area. One way to recognize this is that people who are very high in this area don't have a lot of facial expression. They might smile, but you can't always tell from their expression whether they're happy or displeased with something. Matt would smile in our meetings, but often he'd just sit there and listen and ponder without expression. At first I thought he didn't like me, but then I realized he's very typical for someone high in steadiness and introspection.

USING THE DISC TO IMPROVE LEADERSHIP

Your assessment results can really help you improve your leadership capacity. Good leaders know themselves, and the assessment helps you know your own behaviors and capacities. It helps you identify your own behaviors and also to see them in others. It helps you see beyond someone's experience and education to their true talents. Whether you're dealing with your own boss or leading the pack, you have better communication with everyone.

The assessment can also point out areas you might want to work on. Let's say your assessment shows that you're low on the steadiness end of things. That's something you might want to try to improve. Even if you decide that this is just who you are and you don't want to work on steadiness, having that insight about yourself can help you. You would know that it's not a good idea for you to take on rush projects, for instance, because they stress you out a lot more than they would someone who's lower on the steadiness scale.

INSIGHT WHEEL

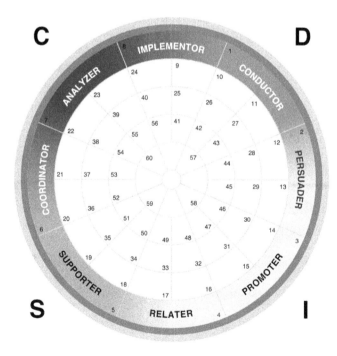

© Target Training International, Ltd.

Groups can also work better if everyone has done the assessment. They will all understand each other's communication styles, for example, and know how to approach their coworkers in the most effective way. We use a tool called an insight wheel (on previous page) to show this graphically to the group. When you look at your position within the wheel, you can see how you connect into the group and how your communication style might be in conflict with another group member. Does that solve the problem? Not instantly, but it shows where the problem lies and puts you on track to deal with it.

One way to resolve the issue is through coaching. For example, depending on the individual, there are certain words and phrases you would never use if you want to communicate. If you're talking with someone who's a D (dominant type) and you say, "We're going to talk about that some more because this is going to require a lot of studying on your part to be able to express this better," that person would just cringe. She doesn't want to hear that; she wants to hear what exactly you don't like about how she expressed herself. If you said to somebody who's high in S (steadiness), "We're going to have a lot of change going on," they would absolutely go crazy. If you said to somebody high in C (compliance), "Give me your educated guess," that person would hate you forever, because Cs don't like to give any educated guesses. What they need to give you is facts, numbers, rules, and figures. What you should be saying to a C instead is, "After analyzing that research, let me know what you come up with." The C is never going to give you a guess, because nothing in his world is gray. Everything is black and white.

From the leadership perspective, having the information from the DISC is invaluable. You use that data and, of course, anything else you know about the person to make the best approach to them, to get the best information from them. The DISC assessment includes communication tips that help you to communicate with people in each category. For example, if you want to communicate with somebody who's high in I (influencing), provide a friendly environment, don't deal with a lot of details, and ask feeling questions. If you're curt, or you control the conversation, or you talk about facts and figures and abstract things, then the person is going to tune you out.

When I coach people who don't get along with the person they work for, I have them take the DISC. Afterward, I show them that page, and I say, "Pick the box that describes your boss." When they do, it tells them exactly how to communicate with that person, which benefits both of them.

DISC AT THE CORPORATE LEVEL

As an individual, you can go to a number of different websites and, for a modest fee, take a short version of the DISC. The information might help you a bit, but it's not at all the same as working with a coach to take the full version and discuss the results with someone highly skilled in interpreting them—and then helping you learn how to adapt what you've just learned.

At the corporate level, having a group of employees take the assessments and then debrief with a trained coach is undeniably the best and most productive way to go. Interpreting and then applying the results is much more complex and can only be effective with the guidance of an expert.

Getting everyone in the group to complete the assessments isn't difficult. I send each person a link, and they do it online at their leisure. It takes no longer than an hour to complete. The key to taking the DISC and the EQ is to be rested, to be well fed, to be in a room all alone where there will be absolutely no distractions—no phones, no email, no knocks on the door—because the least little distraction can skew the results.

In my extensive experience with corporate clients, I find that about three-quarters of the people scheduled to take the assessment contact me and say, "I don't think that assessment is going to tell us much." After they take it and get the results, they say, "I was looking through what you sent me, and it is so true. I don't understand it all, but I think it's true."

WHEN TO ASSESS

I recommend doing DISC and EQ assessments on a regular basis for everyone in the company—it's just good management. More often, however, I find that clients bring me in to use the tools for solving a workplace conflict or problem. When it's crisis time, having the assessment information can be really helpful.

Sometimes I get called in because there's somebody on the team who's not getting along or not functioning well. Usually, I can help that person do better. And occasionally, it prompts that person to just leave. Either way, it's forward progress.

I had a client call me in to work with just one employee. She turned out to be really delightful. As soon as I met her, I knew what the problem was. It wasn't her. It was that everybody else in that company was more of a gray person. This lady was very black and white—very C for compliant. The company is not a black-and-white company. I said to her, "Do you enjoy working there?"

She replied, "Yes, because it's close to home, and I like my hours, and I like my coworkers."

I said, "Okay, but do you like what your mission is?"

She admitted, "I really wish there were more rules. I mean, things change from client to client." That's why everybody in the company was always annoyed with her. She was always questioning everything because she needed to be compliant with the rules—but there weren't any black-and-white rules at this company.

I pointed out, "So do you think your talents would be better used in a company where maybe you were working in the black and white, you were establishing rules or you were writing manuals or maybe you were in a hospital where you were writing protocols? She said, "Well, I love doing that sort of work, but I don't like their hours." I knew the job just wasn't a good fit for her, no matter how much we worked on communications. From working with me, the employee came to realize that as well. I put her in touch with some people and, in the end, she left for a job writing manuals for another company—a perfect fit for her black-and-white approach.

Case Study:
Team Assessments

I recently did a team assessment for the accounting department of a large corporation. Everybody did their assessments; I got all the results and reviewed them. The next step was to do one-on-one discussions of the results with each person. It can take up to two hours per person to debrief—the information is very detailed.

When I finished the individual sessions and everyone had a chance to think about their assessments, it was time to bring the group together. The goal of group discussions is to help them understand how what they've learned about themselves can be applied to working together and communicating better.

The group session took a couple of hours. We focused in on key things, such as where everybody fits on the insight wheel and words to use with various people.

Every corporate manager who was skeptical about the assessments at first has always said to me afterward, "Wow, that was incredibly worthwhile." After the initial sessions, I'm almost always brought back in on a regular basis to go deeper into emotional intelligence training. I often do monthly refreshers with my clients. I also do workshops on topics such as how to deal with difficult people or time management and procrastination. Because the employees have done the assessments and understand who they are in terms of their behaviors, motivators, and emotional intelligence level—we refer back to that information during those workshops. If there's been a lot of turnover in a department over the course of a year or two, I recommend doing the assessments again so the new people have the same information.

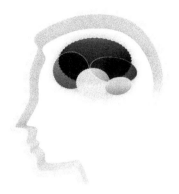

CHAPTER 4

The Value of EQ Training for Leaders

We know from EQ and DISC assessments that most people have a couple of areas where they're strong and a couple where they're weak. When I work with people to prepare them for leadership positions or improve their leadership skills, we focus on the two areas that are lowest. I might have a young executive whose motivation and self-regulation are high, but his empathy and self-awareness are low. We can improve those.

I'll give you an example. I once worked with a successful business owner named Sally who scored very low on every aspect of EQ. On a scale of 1 to 10, she was 2 or 3 in every category. I was stumped about where to begin. We decided to work on her lowest two: self-awareness and self-regulation. Her problems with self-regulation were readily apparent to me—she had no control over her facial expressions. She'd never win at poker, and if looks could kill, she'd be in prison. But she's a good example of how EQ skills can be taught.

I worked with Sally on a set of daily exercises for self-regulation. Whenever someone says something to her, she just wants to tell them the truth right away. She's a black-and-white person in a numbers-oriented, black-and-white business, so her response tends to be along the lines of, "You're wrong, and here's the way it is." That's not the way to get along with people. So we worked on slowing down her responses. She's an introvert, which means she tends to think before she speaks anyway, so this was a good approach for her. I told Sally, "Pause a little bit longer than you normally would." Then I told her, "Pretend I'm telling you what to say."

For some reason, that works for her because she says, "You always say things so politely to people, but yet, you get your point across." She pretends I'm a bug in her ear and asks herself, what would I tell her to say? That has helped her with self-regulation quite a bit. In fact, when we repeated the assessments after working together for about six months, we could see definite improvement in that area.

For other people who have trouble with self-regulation, we might work on different approaches. For some, we work on excusing oneself from the situation to get a drink of water or use the bathroom. That gives them a chance to gather their thoughts rather than just saying whatever first comes to mind. Someone low in self-regulation can be impulsive and might act on impulse as opposed to using thought-provoking statements.

I have a client who goes nuts when vendors show up late on the job site. He used to just blast them with angry emails full of nasty language. We've been working on using better language. Now he's not cursing in the email. Instead, he's saying, "I'm not going to do this with you anymore, and this is unacceptable." So, we've made progress, but now the next step will be to use thought-provoking questions with these vendors, such as, "How can I help you be more efficient in your job?" or "How can I help it be easier for you to get on the site sooner?" It's baby steps with him because his self-regulation is so incredibly low, and he's very impulsive. Yet he's the top producer in his industry.

EQ WORKSHOPS

EQ workshops are an effective tool for making a team more productive and collaborative. When a company hires me to do a workshop, everyone involved receives a link to the EQ assessment. When they've all taken it and I've reviewed the results, we have a workshop that usually runs about two hours. We go through the assessments and discuss what each person is going to improve upon. In some cases, but not always, we talk how they're going to hold each other accountable. Sometimes having your teammates hold you accountable makes people angry. It depends on the team. Oftentimes, it's me holding them accountable.

When I do this with smaller businesses, all the key players participate, and they learn to hold each other accountable. In a recent case, I was brought in because one of the partners was not performing well. He was the company's main sales producer, but he had low self-regulation, low self-awareness, and low social skills. We did the workshop, and he recognized what he needed to work on, but two months later, he left the company. He just didn't like learning that much about himself—he decided to leave rather than respond to what he learned from the EQ assessment. His partners were relieved to see him go voluntarily.

In my experience, it's not uncommon for people to leave a company after looking at those five metrics. The assessment helps them recognize why they are stressed or unhappy and, in some cases, they realize they can never be happy in the environment they're in. Often, the company is relieved that the employee has come to this decision on their own.

In most cases, though, the assessments and workshops help pinpoint difficulties and find good solutions. I'll work with low-performing people once a week to help them improve. Some of them are being considered for promotion to higher levels, so they're motivated to succeed.

DON'T WAIT FOR A PROBLEM

One thing I've learned from years of working with companies is that all too often, by the time I get called in, the situation is near or even at a crisis point. Within every organization, you have all kinds of stressors. When the stressors get bad or go unresolved, suddenly people are missing work for a variety of reasons. Emotional stress certainly takes a toll on physical health, but when people are emotionally balanced and their environment is emotionally balanced, they're going to miss less work. By doing regular EQ evaluations and workshops, your teams are going to sync better. There's going to be a lot more teamwork and cohesiveness. The workshops make your groups stronger and will help to avoid a crisis down the road.

Within every group or organization, there's always room for improvement, even when many people have high EQ. A good example is a high-end financial planner I work with. His EQ is one of the highest I've ever seen—yet he's a terrible listener. At our appointments, we work on his listening skills. I challenge him the whole time with listening skills and empathy. His EQ is high, and he's very successful. Like many successful people, however, he wants to be even better. We've been working on this for a year and a half, and he's definitely improving.

Company EQ workshops and individual coaching are definitely good investments and not just for high-level executives or fast-track trainees. Better EQ helps everybody, including an administrative person at the front desk. That person may not command a high salary, but he or she is also the first impression of your organization for customers or clients. You want that person to have good communication skills and to be happy in the job.

According to the International Coach Federation (coachfederation.org), the return on investment for EQ training is high. If you hire me to help your employees with emotional intelligence, you'll earn back 86 percent of the money you spend. It will come back to you in better productivity, less absenteeism, better communication, improved effectiveness, better work/life balance, and many other ways. Nineteen percent of the companies surveyed said their return on investment in EQ coaching was over 50 times what they spent. The average ROI was seven times what they spent.

Any time you can keep employees and develop them versus hiring new people, you're going to save a minimum of $35,000 a year on up, depending on the level of the person. When you get to the six-figure employees, you could easily save double that. When you compare those costs to the costs of doing EQ training, the savings are very obvious. And of course, you can't really put a price on an improved workplace atmosphere and happier employees.

When there's already a problem at a company and I get called in, I love it. The more dysfunctional the situation, the more I like it. Any coach can work with a high achiever. High achievers are easy. They're always going to show up with their homework done. They're always going to do what you ask them to do. They're going to do it on time, and the coaching is always going to make them show their very best. Working with a group of low achievers is more challenging and more interesting. Making them better is extremely satisfying for a coach. When you develop the emotional intelligence of a group, the work environment improves, becoming more emotionally balanced because everybody is working on themselves. When you've got everybody working on a particular thing, then the lowest common denominator rises. If everybody's low-scoring EQ is coming up a bar, then the whole team is going to be better. That's what I like to accomplish.

Good leaders become better leaders through EQ training. That doesn't mean they become superstars. It means they get better across the board. When we feel we've got a handle on what we struggle with, even if we haven't mastered it, we perform better. Our attitude is better.

CHOOSING AN EFFECTIVE EQ TRAINING PROGRAM

Employers have a lot of options for finding EQ training. I recommend using a well-established program, such as the TriMetrix assessments, that shows results with history and validation. Also look for a program that is regularly updated and improved, as the TriMetrix program is each year. The provider—a coach like me—should be certified by the company and trained in administering and interpreting the assessments. I'm certified by TTI, the company that provides the TriMetrix program. The training was pretty intensive, and they stay on top of me to maintain my certification through continuing education.

When it comes to hiring a provider to do the assessments and work with the employees on the results, look for the personal touch. You want someone with a small staff who will be available personally to pay real attention to your needs. You want your employees to develop a good relationship with the coach. They may end up revealing their deepest feelings to the coach, which can give them the freedom to move on and have a productive life, but only if they feel they can trust her. They won't feel that way if they think they're just a number in a file.

A good coach can coach anyone in any field. It truly doesn't matter if the coach has experience in a particular industry. We work on skills, not functions, and skills are across the board. Someone with coaching experience could really help coach the sales staff, for instance, without ever being in sales. The coaching wouldn't be about how to be better at sales. It would be about how to be better listeners, how to have more empathy, and how to be more motivated and self-regulated.

Because I'm extensively trained in intrinsic methodology and coaching, people who come to me often say, "You're so very different from my other coach." The reason they say that is because this methodology is much deeper than coaching methodologies that are more directive, along the lines of, "Here's how you're going to do this. Here's what you're going to do. Here's how you're going to do it." My approach is intrinsic—the person or group being coached gets to decide what it is that they need. Let's say a manager says, "I want my employees to be more motivated or I want more cohesiveness in the work environment." As soon as they decide what they want for themselves, then it's easy for them to come up with what they're going to do to get it, rather than me telling them. So because I coach that way, they often feel heard more than they ever have before. It's their decision how to move forward.

Assessments are valuable, but when a client does all the check-boxes and everything the coach recommended, if they never really addressed what they wanted, then they're just spinning their wheels. What they really want is peace of mind, and you don't get that from checking a bunch of boxes.

The way I coach is I listen to what my clients say, but I also listen to what they don't say. When they say, "My wife and I are fighting all the time," or "My boss is mad at me every morning," or "I feel moody in the morning," I know something else is going on. Maybe it's an addiction or a bad habit, or maybe they're depressed. I'm not qualified to address those issues, but I can certainly recognize them and refer the client to appropriate professional help.

Case Study:
Improving Self-Regulation

People who are struggling with leadership issues can improve through EQ training. One example is my client Joseph C. He attained his job through family connections, so he gets more scrutiny than someone else in his position might. But he also had problems because his EQ is low in some areas. There's a saying, "Life is 10 percent what happens to you and 90 percent how you react to it." Joseph was a 90 percent reactor. He was always reacting to everything. If you looked at him crossways, he thought he did something wrong, probably because he did. Clearly, his self-regulation and his social skills needed work. We had a lot to do, but Joseph was eager to learn. He was unhappy in his work and his life and really wanted to do something about it.

About 18 months after we began working together, I was at an art event and overheard two women talking about someone. One said, "I don't know what's happened to him. It is like God came down and did some work on him. He's just a different person."

I realized that I knew one of the women: she worked at Joseph's company. She saw me and said, "Hey, you're a coach. What do you say to someone who's stopped behaving like a jerk?"

I thought fast and said, "You could say 'I don't know what you've been doing lately, but you just seem a lot happier.' That way you're not addressing the way he's acting. You're just addressing him as a person."

Coaching in EQ made Joseph generally just happier and easier to be around. But it also got him, after ten years at the company, a raise and the Employee of the Year award. Some of my clients don't talk about our coaching, but Joseph is so happy with the results from working with me that he tells everybody.

CHAPTER 5

Improving Leadership Skills with EQ Training

E Q training helps people in leadership positions do better by helping them with the five core skills:

- Self-awareness
- Self-regulation
- Empathy
- Motivation
- Social skills

Self-awareness, self-regulation, and motivation fall into the category of intrapersonal emotional intelligence. Intrapersonal means what goes on inside of you as you experience day-to-day happenings or events.

Empathy and social skills fall into the category of interpersonal emotional intelligence. Interpersonal means what goes on between you and others.

LEARNING SELF-AWARENESS

The first solution to any problem is self-awareness. It's not a magic cure, though. As soon as you become aware of what you're doing, you may continue to make the same mistakes, but at least you'll be aware. And maybe the next time, you won't make that mistake. Self-awareness may help you stop yourself at the last second.

As current and future leaders become aware of their emotional intelligence strengths and weaknesses, they'll learn more about how they're perceived by others. Being more self-aware will also help with their passion, their intensity, and their hard work, and, once they recognize this, fewer problems will arise.

An indicator of someone low in self-awareness is when someone doesn't understand the correlation between her emotions and her behavior. She may be behaving negatively and have no clue as to why. It could be simply because she got stuck in traffic or her dog ran off and made her late for work or her first appointment of the day canceled. Or perhaps she just woke up feeling grumpy. No matter the underlying cause, her emotions are affecting her work in a negative way, but because she's low in self-awareness she doesn't realize it.

I teach my clients some simple ways to become more self-aware:

- Set a timer for five different random times during the day. When the timer goes off, write down in your journal or notebook how you feel. Look at your responses at the end of the day. Try to see how your mood impacted, or was impacted by, what happened that day.

- Make a list of your strengths and weaknesses. Then ask a family member or trusted friend/advisor to describe your strengths and weaknesses to you. Compare the two lists. If you see big differences between the two lists, chances are your self-awareness is skewed. Create an action plan to develop your areas of weakness.

- Note in your journal how you responded to significant situations throughout the day. At the end of the day, review your reactions. Were they appropriate or applicable? If not, give some thought to how they could have been better.

- After practicing self-awareness for a month, you've probably improved in some areas. Reward yourself with something enjoyable, like going fishing, having a mani-pedi, seeing a movie, starting a new book, taking a walk on the beach— anything that's fun for you. Your brain registers the reward and makes you want to continue to improve.

Part of my job is to teach you how to recover from saying the wrong thing due to lack of self-awareness. You can say, "Wait a minute, you know what? I didn't mean to say that. Let me rephrase that." Or, if you've already gotten into a conversation, you can retract it and say, "I'd like to retract part of our conversation. Let me elaborate further on what I meant." There are all kinds of ways to diffuse the toxicity or the negative behavior as you're learning how to not use it.

LEARNING SELF-REGULATION

Self-regulation is the ability to control or redirect disruptive impulses and moods and the propensity to suspend judgment—to think before acting. People low in self-regulation can be seen as cold or uncaring, because often they suppress their emotions. They may even minimize the influence their emotions have on outcomes—they don't realize emotions impact their decisions. In some situations, they may not show emotions even when emotions are appropriate.

For learning better self-regulation, I coach my clients to

- In conversations, listen first, pause, and only then respond.
- Be consistently committed to not interrupting others.
- In difficult or overwhelming situations, step away for a bit before responding. When your self-regulation is low, your initial response is rarely positive.

LEARNING MOTIVATION

People high in motivation pursue their goals consistently and with energy. People low in motivation are usually comfortable with the status quo. You will often hear them say phrases such as, "I just don't feel like trying," or "What if I fail again?"

I help my clients improve their motivation by helping them define what they are truly passionate about and why that is important to them. Once they understand their motivation, then we can work on some ways to improve it:

- Set specific goals with dates for achievement.
- Spend some time every day visualizing the outcome of what you are trying to achieve.
- Read articles and books that inspire you; memorize inspiring quotes. Movies are good for inspiration, too: I like *Legally Blonde, Rocky, Flashdance,* and *Forrest Gump.*

LEARNING EMPATHY

Steve Jobs is a solid example of a great leader who was hugely lacking in empathy but was high in self-awareness. Jobs had terrible personality traits. He was narcissistic. He had a great imagination, but he was a perfectionist. He was obsessive. He was great at creation and innovation, but he just wasn't a good people person. The crucial point is, he knew it. He chose people to work with who did have those skills. Tim Cook, who is now Apple's CEO, is calm and consistent and never raises his voice. Jobs and Cook made a good team, and Apple has been able to stay innovative and successful after Jobs's death.

To help someone develop empathy, I'll ask him or her to watch interactions between other people and make notes about them in a journal. In other words, watch the body language of the people in the conversation and observe what they're experiencing. A good place to do this is in a public area, like the food court of a shopping mall.

Let's say you're watching a couple have an argument—the man bought something the woman didn't want him to buy. It's easier for someone who's not personally involved to see the impact negative communication causes just by looking at body language. When we review the notes later, I'll say, "Do you see where shaming people or scolding employees or even talking down to someone can be so debilitating?" The response is something like, "Yeah, I felt sorry for that poor guy." From there, I can say, "Possibly, when you're talking to your employees and you're wound up because you scored low in empathy, there's a strong possibility that you do the same thing."

To develop empathy, I'll encourage the individual I'm coaching to work on understanding body language even further. I'll ask them to say something to me as if I were an employee and observe my body language as I take in the message. I'll ask, "How did I feel when you were telling me that?" People who are low in empathy can't really tell if someone is feeling an emotion. They'll say, "I think you felt fine," when I was really demonstrating shame or guilt. They don't pick up cues from spoken and body language. It goes the other way, too—they have to learn about their own body language. I'm a fidgeter, for example. I don't want someone to think that because I'm fidgeting I'm not interested in what they have to say. Because I'm self-aware, I make an extra effort to avoid fidgeting when it could be misinterpreted.

LEARNING SOCIAL SKILLS

Learning to speak only after you pause and think about what you have just heard is a crucial social skill. I teach clients who need to work on their social skills to wait four seconds before speaking. This gives them time to think before, not after, saying something. I actually have to teach some clients to mentally count off the four seconds.

People with low social skills aren't always aware of being wrong about something or making a mistake. Because their social skills are low, when they do know they've made a mistake, their ego and pride get wrapped up in it and they find it hard to acknowledge the error. To remedy this, I have those clients agree that any time they're wrong about something, they have to immediately admit they were wrong, apologize, and move forward. We do this for a week. It's really hard for someone with low social skills.

It could be as simple as saying, "I interrupted you—sorry." That's a common problem. During a meeting, a person with low social skills may just blurt out his thoughts, not even considering that someone else is speaking. When they realize they've done that, I'll train them to pause for a moment and then say, "I'm sorry, I didn't let you finish," and then shut up and let the other person finish.

Another thing that people with low social skills struggle with is remembering people's names. I teach them memory techniques—there are a lot of these, and at least one of them is bound to work.

Sometimes, people with low social skills are not good at team-oriented tasks or events. Joining a professional organization or a work team where they must participate and do things as a team helps with that. A group that helps a lot of my clients is Toastmasters. This wonderful organization (I've been an active member for years) is very good at improving your public speaking ability, which can really help with social skills.

In my early years as a hotshot salesperson, I was number two in the country for sales, but as soon as I had to give a presentation, I was a hot mess. My boss suggested I join Toastmasters. I almost fainted the first time I gave a speech, and the second time, and then the third time. But suddenly, I started liking it. About six months in, I won Table Topics, where you speak impromptu for a minute. Then I won at the annual local event, which meant I got to go to the city-wide level. I became very good at it. Then they voted me in as president of my chapter. To this day, I thank my boss for making me do it. As a leader, you must be able to speak convincingly without forewarning.

I worked with a manager who was low in a lot of EQ areas. He applied for leadership positions in his company four or five different times but never got them. Part of the selection process was a panel interview. The panel made him feel like he was on stage and he would bomb. He knew all the information; he just couldn't verbalize it. He couldn't answer their questions well—he would go off on a tangent because he would be so nervous.

I worked with him for four months on interviewing. I had him pretend I was a panel. I would pretend I was a man and then a woman. I would throw the questions at him and deliberately try to make him nervous. All the practice paid off—at the next interview panel, he got the position.

THE PAYOFF

The payoff to a company for paying attention to EQ training is lower worker turnover. People who leave a company aren't usually leaving the company—they're leaving their manager or leader. They leave because of a bad boss. The better the leader, the higher his or her EQ, the more they're working on themselves—the better the chances that they'll be able to keep an effective team in place. A manager who has a stable life because he's more emotionally intelligent won't be bringing his personal problems to the office. That manager has more emotional energy available to be more in tune with the employees. The payoff is incredible, both personally and professionally.

When employees don't feel recognized or appreciated or valued, they will leave. A manager who is higher in EQ, especially empathy and social skills, is going to remember to thank the employees or reward them with something that matters to them. That motivates employees.

If a company can figure out what frustrates its employees, something can be done. Maybe a manager is micromanaging or spouts off when something goes wrong. Maybe the company isn't providing the employees with the guidance they need and deserve. The assessments tell the leaders what's going on and makes them more aware. If managers are held accountable to a coach, they'll be more apt to do the things they need to do to improve and less apt to lose their employees. If you do the whole, complete assessment of everyone in the company, you then know what motivates each individual employee. As a leader or manager, you'll know how to motivate them in the most effective way. If money isn't a big motivator for an employee but knowledge is, then they're going to be happier if you send them to a training course than if you just hand them extra money in their paycheck. It's a win-win.

Case Study:
The Guys Learn to Work Together

I recently worked with a group of six midlevel managers to help them be better leaders and work better as a team. The group was all men—and let's just say egos abounded. The company president brought me in because he felt there was a great deal of animosity and a lot of one-upsmanship in the group. The lack of cohesiveness was significantly impacting their performance.

When we did the DISC and EQ assessments, we found that most of them were low in empathy and self-regulation. For the group, I decided to focus on those two areas and also work with the individuals in one-on-one sessions. In the one-on-ones, the problem became very apparent. As I met with each person, he would say, "He does this. He does that." It was all about the other person and finger pointing. No one was taking responsibility for anything.

When I was brought in, the group was reluctant to work with me. But on the training and debriefing day, they had a blast. They were laughing and pointing fingers at each other. It was hilarious. There was so much laughter in the room that somebody who worked at the company heard it and came by and said, "I wish I had been able to do this."

The training helped—there's no more finger pointing. There's a whole lot more teamwork. They tread cautiously now, but they do have to be reminded by each other. Sometimes one has to say to another, "I don't think I did that wrong." Instead of getting defensive or angry, the other guy is now more likely to say, "Oh yes, I know it was me." When clients come in, these six are more in tune with helping the client, as opposed to arguing over who's making the sale.

I still go in and work with three people there. I also do tune-ups with the group every month or so to keep them on track.

CHAPTER 6

Improving Self-Awareness
for Better Leadership

Good leaders are self-aware. They know when they're reacting emotionally and can usually stop themselves before they say or do something harmful. They may not always succeed, but even then, they're self-aware enough to know when they've made a mistake. If you're not self-aware, then your ability to lead is diminished.

When you're not self-aware, you're constantly reacting to things employees and colleagues do wrong or even things they did right but they didn't do perfectly. You're reacting. You're flying off the handle. Maybe you roll your eyes when something goes wrong. You're not even aware of it. EQ in the self-awareness area is all about how you react and how you anticipate the things that are going wrong.

If you have self-awareness, then you're going to know how you're feeling. You're going to know why you're feeling that way. You're going to know your personal strengths and your limitations. You're going to have a decent sense of your self-worth and capabilities.

But if you're low in self-awareness, then you're going to have low self-esteem. You're going to second-guess yourself. You don't know what your strengths and weaknesses are, so you won't hire accordingly. You won't necessarily hire a team that has a balance of strengths. You'll probably hire people who are all strong in the same area instead of looking for people who complement each other.

DIVERSITY IN THE WORKPLACE

When coaches talk about diversity in the workplace, we mean not just different shapes and sizes and colors but also the many diverse skills people have. A leader with good self-awareness, especially if he's had some EQ training, is good at recognizing the value of diversity in giving the workplace a good mix of skills. Recognizing diversity also helps a leader to enable every employee to find the best way to get his or her job done.

A leader who's low in self-awareness is almost always also low in self-esteem. Because of that, the leader will be reluctant to hire somebody who's strong in an area she's not strong in for fear that the new person will outshine her. That means she doesn't put together a strong team with a good range of skills. The team becomes unbalanced.

When I ran a sales team, I made sure everybody on the team had a different skill set. They definitely all had a skill that I wasn't necessarily good at, such as computer skills. I made sure we had somebody on our team who was really fast and savvy. When we went out to do presentations, she could set up the computer and projector in five minutes and get it up and running even if she ran into a problem. If it had been up to me, I would have fumbled through for 30 minutes.

LIMITING YOUR LEADERSHIP ABILITY

Lack of self-awareness can really limit your ability to lead. If you recognize yourself in any of the descriptions below, you must learn to increase your self-awareness if you want to be a truly effective leader:

- *You're indecisive.* As a leader, you face deadlines and the need for good, fast decisions. If you lack self-awareness, then you may not even realize that you're indecisive. You might think that calling the president of the company to get his input on something is the right thing to do. In fact, you're just annoying him while also telling him you can't make decisions. I teach my clients to be self-aware enough to realize when they're being indecisive and show them how to take steps to get to a decision. The approach that works best for people with low self-awareness is often to make a pro and con list, pick the choice that has more pros, and go with it. If it turns out to be the wrong decision, so be it. Likely, nobody is going to die from it.

- *You can't monitor your feelings.* If you lack self-awareness, then you don't know how you feel, or if you do know, you don't know why. You think, *I'm disturbed because what's in front of me isn't working.* In fact, that's not what you're disturbed about. You're disturbed about something else—maybe the argument you had with your spouse that morning. It has nothing to do with the frozen computer in front of you.

- *You blow up at people.* If people are hungry at work or they're tired, they're more apt to blow up, especially if they're low in self-awareness. There's no connection between your emotions and the behavior that triggers them. They can be skewed.

- *You don't have rapport with your colleagues and employees.* If you don't understand your own moods and emotions, then you're definitely not going to be aware enough to understand those of your colleagues or the effect your behavior has on others. It's harder to be inclusive of someone who's like that. They're just exhausting to be around. You don't even want to run into them in the break room, much less go out for a drink. If you lack rapport with your employees, they'll quit.

- *You're insensitive to the people around you in terms of skill diversity.* Usually when people are lacking in self-awareness, they seek out others who are like them. They look for the same mind-set, instead of different skills. I often see teams where everybody is the same. I even worked once with a company where everybody there was brunette. I said to the owner, "You asked me the last time we had lunch if I knew anybody who'd be interested in a job here. I'm just wondering, if that person was a blonde, would she be refused?"

She replied, "Of course not."

I said, "I just find it odd that everyone who works here is brunette." She was unaware of it. She was discriminating without even knowing it, but she was also hurting her business.

- *You're not trusted by upper management.* When you're low in self-esteem and low in self-awareness, it's hard to trust you because you don't even trust yourself. If you're indecisive as well, or if people in your department tend to quit a lot, then they'll trust you even less. You can't really expect anybody else to trust you or promote you.

- *You might be a workaholic.* You're so unaware of your own emotions and drives that you overwork, but you're not more productive. I'm a prime example of not realizing that I was overdoing it and that being a workaholic was making me sick. I overworked for years and didn't understand why I was so tired and worn out. More than two decades ago, I had a thriving career in sales. I was young and energetic but not particularly mature or self-aware. I was so eager to achieve and be the top salesperson in the country that I worked myself into sickness. Had I been more self-aware, I would have known that I was getting sick. All the symptoms were there, but I just wasn't listening. Fortunately, I was able to make a full recovery. What I learned from that experience is that no job, no credential, no number-one-in-the-country is worth your health. Today, when I'm already booked with clients and someone says, "Can you please get me in that day?" and I see that my calendar is at a maximum, I say no. I know serving them isn't really serving them if I'm not serving myself.

WAYS TO IMPROVE YOUR SELF-AWARENESS

You can definitely improve your self-awareness. I recommend working with a coach who can use assessments to evaluate your strengths and weaknesses and give you constructive feedback. The great football coach Tom Landry once said, "A coach is someone who tells you what you don't want to hear, who has you see what you don't want to see, so you can be who you have always known you could be."

If you don't want to go that route, try describing your strengths and weaknesses to a close family member or trusted friend. That way, you'll know what your weaknesses are, and you can improve your ability to self-assess. You can compare their feedback to your own assessment.

Case Study:
Learning Self-Awareness

Because she lacks self-awareness, Jennifer C. isn't much liked at her company. She can be tactless and abrupt but doesn't realize how much her behavior upsets her coworkers and makes upper management reluctant to promote her.

I was asked to coach Jennifer on improving work relationships. We did assessments that revealed her self-awareness issues to her. I gave her homework assignments that she took very seriously. She was able to become more aware of how she annoys people. She also became more aware of how she feels, which helped her understand when she should interact with people and when she shouldn't.

After I had been working with Jennifer for several months, the president of the company told me, "You know, I'm thinking about giving Jennifer an additional role. I really trust her now, and I really feel she can handle it."

"Really?" I said. "What's changed?"

He said, "Well, basically she's not upsetting everybody anymore. She seems to be more in tune with the mood of the meetings. She understands her emotions. She's not flying off the handle."

Given that six months earlier her boss had been thinking of firing Jennifer, I was relieved. Jennifer is still one of my best examples of how someone's self-awareness can really change her circumstances for the better.

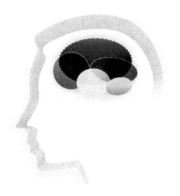

CHAPTER 7

Managing Emotions in a
Leadership Position

In emotional intelligence terms, managing your emotions falls into the category of self-regulation, one of the intrapersonal areas. Self-regulation is the ability to control or redirect disruptive impulses and moods and the propensity to suspend judgment and think before acting. When you have high self-regulation, you handle stress well. You're good at controlling your emotions, especially in high-stress situations, and you work well under pressure. You could sit through a very stressful meeting and keep a poker face, no matter how rattled you feel inside.

Self-regulation is a big problem for a lot of people, though. In our lives we've had to go through a lot of experiences and traumas, big and small. They make us what we are, but they leave their mark in the form of triggers—words, gestures, actions, even smells that can remind us of bad experiences and make us lose self-regulation. We all have some triggers, but for people who don't have good coping skills, a trigger can cause an emotional reaction that makes them angry or anxious or sad or some other negative feeling. When people respond to a trigger, it's not that they're bad people. It's just that they've had experiences that trigger them and make them react, often inappropriately.

There was a time in my life when a well-meaning friend would always say to me, "Here's what you need to do. You need to blah, blah, blah." Any time you tell someone what they *need* to do, it's bossy, it's directive, it's controlling, and it's manipulative. Because I so hated hearing my friend say that to me, to this day, if someone says to me, "What you need to do …," I completely tune them out. If they say to me, "What I would like for you to do," that's fine. Or "What I suggest you do," or "In my experience what I've done," I'm totally fine with it. The first time somebody throws that word "need," I'm tuning them out. I know it's a trigger, and I know what happens when I hear it, so I can try to react more positively, but it still bugs me every time.

I worked with a young manager who often had to work with the older executives. They would call him boy because he was so much younger than them. He hated it. It would just set him off. He completely lost it when he told me about it. I explained to him, "For that generation of men, that's just their terminology. It has nothing to do with them thinking you're inferior or you're not smart enough or you're too young. It's more to do with their own terminology. You can't change them." Since we worked on it, now when people say it, he laughs. It tickles him that it ever bothered him.

Sometimes actions are triggers. I had a boss once who needed her morning routine. She wanted to get to her office, unload her briefcase, get her computer turned on, and get her coffee before any of us approached her.

I didn't pick up on that at first. I'd approach her as she walked in the door. She would glare at me, and I would think, *Why is she in such a bad mood?* In fact, all she wanted was to sit down and get organized before dealing with the day's work. I was intruding on her little personal, private morning ritual, but I didn't realize it. I was the trigger that made her snap at me. One day, I finally asked her. I said, "When I approach you with these questions, you seem to be annoyed."

She said, "When you approach me and I haven't even sat down yet, yes." It was good for me to be aware.

SELF-REGULATION BUILDS EMPLOYEE CONFIDENCE

Employees feel confident when the boss has high self-regulation. They know that if they bring you a problem, you're not going to scream at them—you're going to find a constructive way to help. There's nothing like a calm leader. A calm leader is awesome to work for because you know no matter what happens, everything is going to be fine.

With self-regulation comes honesty and integrity. There's nothing better than working for someone with those qualities. People with good self-regulation usually take responsibility if they're wrong. They're not going to fire you on the spot if you admit to a mistake.

And they're okay with employees coming up with new ideas. They're not threatened by it.

LACK OF SELF-REGULATION

A lack of self-regulation can severely hinder your ability to lead. If you're good at managing your emotions, then you're more even-tempered and less likely to feel anxious and irritable. Managers with low EQ can't control their emotions. They have temper tantrums and extreme responses that alienate others. Employees don't respect a leader who can't manage emotions, and they tend to work around them rather than approach them with issues.

When I'm working with a client who's low in self-regulation, we work on ways to handle the emotions that come up when they're agitated by a trigger, especially if the trigger is someone they work with. Removing yourself from the situation or delaying is often very helpful. You can go outside and walk around the block or go to the rest room or for a coffee break. You can simply say, "Excuse me, I need to take care of something for a minute. I'll be right back."

If you really think you're going to lose it, say "Let's talk about this later this afternoon," or "That's not a priority for me right now—I have other things I need to look at first."

ANGER MANAGEMENT

Someone who's angry a lot usually has problems with self-regulation, to the point where they can't be an effective leader. Fortunately, anger management is a skill that can be taught.

Most people with anger issues have never been taught coping mechanisms that help them defuse their anger or distract themselves from it. I teach my clients the four Ds to help them manage anger:

- Drink water
- Delay the impulse to react
- Distract yourself
- Deep breaths

I can't stress enough the value of leaving the scene as a way to manage anger. If you feel yourself getting angry, say, "Excuse me for a minute. I'll be right back. I'm just walking outside." Take a walk outside or at least out of the office area to delay your anger impulse and distract yourself from how you feel. Once you get away, have a drink of water and take deep breaths. Go back inside only when you feel you're under control again.

HANDLING ANXIETY

The four Ds also work really well for handling anxiety. If you feel yourself being overwhelmed with anxiety, get out of there. Take a walk, have some water, take deep breaths. You can't necessarily delay your anxiety, but what you can do is you ask yourself, "In this situation, what's the worst that can happen?" If you answer that honestly, then you'll realize that nothing much at all is likely to happen. Nobody is going to steal your child. Nobody is going to beat you up. Nobody is going to burn your house down. Really, nothing that bad can happen. You're just getting worked up. You can't get a handle on your emotions because you're low in self-regulation.

I teach my clients some simple techniques for relieving anxiety when they start to feel stressed. Feeling pressured because you're running behind on a big project or a deadline is looming is a major cause of office anxiety. Good time management is a great anxiety preventer. I have a really good, easy-to-use time management tool on my website (www.CoachingByKarenNutter.com), go to resource tab and click on coaching downloads.

Mindfulness is another good way to relieve anxiety. I sometimes teach people how to meditate or refer them to www.relaxationre-sponse.org, a good website that teaches the basics of meditation. The reason people start doing mindfulness or meditation is because they're anxious or they're perfectionists and they want to calm down. Of course, the last thing they need is to think that they're not doing meditation or mindfulness perfectly. The main thing I teach them is, however you're doing it *is* perfect. It doesn't need to be more perfect than that. Nobody's checking up on the quality of your meditation.

For meditating, all you need to do is find a quiet spot where you're not going to be interrupted for 20 minutes or so. This can be hard, but it's manageable. If you can't find 20 minutes, even one minute is enough to get you started.

The idea of meditation is to push other thoughts away and just focus on right now. Especially at first, people do have other thoughts. Keep a pen and paper beside you and just write down whatever thoughts come to you, and then go back to your meditation. Otherwise, you're just going to keep obsessing about those things that you want to write down and do.

If you're having what I call mind chatter—countless distracting thoughts—pretend it's a sunny day. The mind chatter is a cloud. As soon as that dark cloud passes, the sun comes out again. As soon as you get rid of that thought, the sun is going to come up and you're back into your meditation.

Today there are phone apps that help you meditate by tracking your time, reminding you to do it, and even sounding a nice, gentle alarm when your time is up. I usually recommend my clients try the Oprah and Deepak Chopra meditations found at www.chopracentermeditation.com, available on CD or as a mobile app. Many of my clients like the Silva guided meditations app for their smartphones.

DEPRESSION

Depression is a common problem. In severe cases, it's obviously a medical condition that must be addressed professionally. People with low self-awareness may not even realize they're suffering from mild depression. They're just going to think the world is too much for them. This is where EQ assessment can be really helpful for personal insight. If you have a tendency toward depression, that will show up in your assessment. You'll be more likely to recognize that you're depressed. If not, hopefully, someone in your life will be brave enough to say, "I think you're down, and you may need help."

SUBSTANCE ABUSE AND ALCOHOLISM

Sometimes, substance abuse or alcoholism can keep talented people from ever achieving their leadership potential. When I recognize the signs in the people I coach, I can gently try to make them aware that they may have a problem. I use a pamphlet called "Is A.A. For You? Twelve Questions Only You Can Answer" (you can find the questions at www.aa.org). If you answer yes to four or more questions, then there's a chance you have a problem with alcohol.

I usually just say, "I have this questionnaire. Would you be willing to look at it?" They're often very open to it. I read the question. I have them say yes or no. I have them count how many yeses they have. Then I read to them what the pamphlet says. If they answer yes to four or more, then I'll say, "It's something you might want to look at. Have you ever thought about this?"

If they say, "No, I've never thought about it. I don't have a problem," then I dismiss it.

If they say, "Yes, it's in my family. I've always known," then I usually say, "Why don't you just go to a meeting and say you're doing a study and you're investigating?" That way, it gets them in the door and on the way to better self-understanding.

Bad stuff happens to us. How well we deal with it shows how well we can lead and who we are. In general, leaders deal with bad things that happen by reframing the situation as disappointing, rather than bad. They appreciate that it's nothing personal; it's just that bad things sometimes happen. They don't let difficult emotions knock them off track. They know no one has ever died from a bad feeling.

Poor self-regulation leads to negative self-talk. When things get tough, people with low self-regulation tend to say negative, self-defeating things to themselves. With a little practice, you can learn to replace negative self-talk with positive, affirming words.

CHANGING YOUR SELF-TALK

It is important to acknowledge that negative self-talk is damaging and counter-productive. With that in mind, for every negative thought, substitute a positive one that's stronger and will get you moving in the right direction.

NEGATIVE TALK	POSITIVE TALK
I'm unworthy	I'm worthy
I'm inadequate	I'm capable
I'm a failure	I'm smart
I'm angry	I'm patient
I'm stupid	I'm accepting of myself
I'm guilty	I'm generous
I can't succeed	I'm successful
I can't get what I want	I acknowledge my accomplishments
I'm helpless	I'm loved
I hate myself	I love and like myself
There's something wrong with me	I am trustworthy
I can't control my thoughts	I consciously choose my thoughts
I lack confidence	I'm confident
I never get it right	I value and appreciate my talents, skills, and abilities
Nothing works for me	I ask for and allow help and support
I don't deserve happiness	I live a joyful life
Nobody understands me	I have close, satisfying relationships

Case Study: Improving Negative Self-Talk

I was asked to do an EQ assessment of an accounting team that just wasn't working well together. When I interviewed the team members, I heard a lot of negative self-talk. The team members got upset with each other easily, blamed each other, and were generally negative about everything, including themselves. When I interviewed Walt F., the team leader, I realized that while the other team members may have had some issues with negativity, Walt had a major problem—and his negativity as a leader was trickling down to his team. I worked with all the team members on replacing negative self-talk with more positive thinking. When I talked with Walt about how he could blow up over trivial issues, we discovered that his inner dialogue was so negative in part because he was going through a difficult divorce.

Over the next six months, I worked with the whole team on improving their self-talk and having a more positive outlook. My coaching gradually helped them become a happier and more cohesive team. What helped almost as much, however, was that Walt got some counseling to help him with his emotional response to his unhappy family situation. As a leader, Walt's self-talk had a big impact on his team. As his negativity gradually improved, his team started to have a more positive outlook as well.

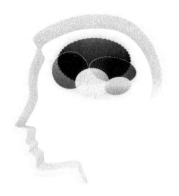

CHAPTER 8

Motivation for Better Leadership

Motivation, as stated earlier, is the passion to work for reasons that go beyond money or status. It's an inclination to pursue goals with energy and persistence, characterized by striving to improve or meet a standard of excellence and aligning yourself with the goals of a group or organization.

People with high motivation quickly act on opportunities and persistently pursue goals despite obstacles and setbacks.

PROCRASTINATION AND MOTIVATION

Procrastination is a huge thief of motivation. Even when people feel extremely passionate about something, if they're procrastinators, it may seem as if they're not motivated, even though they actually are. Their motivation is being covered up by the procrastination.

Using my time management tool (see chapter 7) can really help with getting past procrastination and getting more done. You can increase your motivation by using the tool to set a specific goal with a milestone and a date for achieving the goal.

A technique I like to use when teaching corporate groups about avoiding procrastination and staying motivated is called if-then. Ask yourself, "If I don't do this now, then what?"

The answer might be, "I'm too tired today," or "It's going to take too much time," or "I'll do this tomorrow," or "It's okay, I'll still have time to do it tomorrow."

Oftentimes, then never comes, or there's something else that's more important. When you find yourself doing if-then a lot, you probably need to look at why you're procrastinating.

Nine times out of ten, it's fear and perfectionism. It's not laziness. People think that procrastinators are lazy, and that's not it at all. They're afraid. Of what? All sorts of things, depending on the person. Afraid of success, afraid of doing it wrong, afraid of maybe they'll get into it and they won't understand everything they need to know. Afraid it may take longer than what they thought. Afraid they may finish it before they think they will, and then they'll have nothing to do at work.

The key with the if-then plan is to put it on a piece of paper and keep it somewhere you can see it. That way, not only is it a visual reminder to push you to do the work, but the very act of writing down the implementation plan will solidify your commitment to do it. If you'll commit five or ten minutes to a project, oftentimes you'll get engaged with it and continue. It's taking that first step that's the hard part.

Another technique is to have an accountability partner. Because if you tell somebody you're going to do something, whether it's a coach or a friend or a coworker, you're more likely to do it.

Another good way to increase motivation is to clarify why your goals are important. Ask yourself not only what are my goals but also why are these my goals? What makes these goals important to me? I suggest working with a coach or a trusted adviser to create some detailed action items to help you work toward your goals. You can set aside a little bit of time every day, even if it's just five minutes, to work on whatever your important goals are. That keeps you motivated. It's kind of like exercising every day. If you're a visual person, then write your goals out and put them in places where you can see them often.

MOTIVATING EMPLOYEES

Highly motivated leaders motivate their employees. They start by creating an open atmosphere that allows people to admit to mistakes without fear. If you're afraid that if you mess up you're going to get into trouble, then you may not be motivated to take the first step in a new project.

Celebrating small accomplishments is a great motivator for employees. Recognition and little gifts and tokens really help. If somebody does something good and you put a congratulatory sticky note on their desk when they're not looking, they get very motivated. They want to get another sticky, coffee gift card, or whatever. A little bit of competition also increases motivation. It doesn't have to be motivation to work harder. Some companies have programs to help employees get healthier and have competitions to see who loses the most weight or walks the most. Days off to do volunteer work in the community are great motivators. So is casual Friday or pizza Thursday. When the leader is the one going out to get the birthday cake for an employee, it's a great motivator. Employees like to know you went out of your way for them.

MATURITY AND LEADERSHIP

Through my work as a coach helping people develop their leadership skills, I've come to see how important it is to be mature—to behave as a responsible adult. I feel so strongly about this that I've put my thoughts into a short essay.

Maturity

Maturity is the ability to tolerate an injustice without wanting to get even.

Maturity is patience. It is the willingness to postpone immediate gratification in favor of the long-term gain.

Maturity is perseverance, sweating out a project in the face of heavy opposition and discouraging setbacks.

Maturity is the capacity to face unpleasantness and frustration, discomfort, and defeat without complaint, collapse, or attempting to find someone to blame.

Maturity is humility. It is being big enough to say, "I was wrong." And, when right, the mature person is able to forego the satisfaction of saying, "I told you so."

Maturity is the ability to evaluate a situation, make a decision, and stick with it.

The immature spend their lives exploring possibilities, then changing their minds.

In the end, they have accomplished nothing.

Maturity means dependability, keeping one's word, coming through in a crisis.

The immature are masters of the alibi. They are confused and disorganized.

Their lives are a maze of broken promises, former friends, unfinished business, and good intentions that never materialized.

Maturity is the art of living in peace with that which we cannot change, having the courage to change that which can be changed and seeking the wisdom to know the difference.

Case Study:
Learning to Handle Anxiety

On an anxiety scale of 0 to 10, my client Jane V. ranged from 6 all the way up to 9 on a daily basis. She constantly felt overwhelmed. She could have one thing on her plate or she could have 20 things on her plate—and she was equally overwhelmed.

The reason she's so anxious and overwhelmed is because she's a perfectionist. When she starts something, the idea that she won't do it perfectly and might get something wrong just paralyzes her. She often simply cannot get started on something. Her perfectionism creates a huge amount of anxiety, which, in turn, creates a huge amount of procrastination and keeps her from managing her time effectively.

Then when it's finally deadline time and she has to do it, she'll be so full of anxiety because the deadline is completely debilitating to her. She gets angry with herself because she's the cause of her own procrastination. In this cycle of emotions, Jane's anxiety goes sky high. She has a heart condition, so then her heart condition escalates. As her heart condition escalates, she has to double her medication. Then she has to go see her heart doctor.

Based on Jane's EQ assessment, this all stems from low motivation, low self-regulation, and low self-awareness.

Because she's not high in self-awareness, she lets herself go too long without eating, which worsens her heart problem. She overcommits because she's a people pleaser, but then she can't please anybody, much less herself. She's off the charts with empathy, so she will be too empathetic and take on too many projects. Then she's just overwhelmed, her anxiety kicks in, and she's a hot mess.

To help Jane, I asked her to commit to only a certain number of appointments a day. That includes doctor's appointments, business appointments, and social appointments. We agreed that she would only take on a certain number of clients.

Because she hadn't been on a vacation in many years, I got Jane to plan a true vacation, not a trip to a conference or a family visit. She scheduled it, and then the day before leaving she called me with extreme anxiety about getting all her packing done. She had four appointments for that day as well. We went through her appointment list and saw that three of the four could be cancelled. I coached her to see that by cancelling them, she would free up her day to pack and tie up loose ends around her house.

Those three appointments Jane cancelled were not even that important; there was only one appointment that was urgent. She was creating her own crisis. We worked on ways to help her realize that crisis and chaos aren't good management techniques, and Jane was able to leave on time for her vacation the next day.

CHAPTER 9

Social Awareness for Leadership

S ocial awareness in EQ terms means empathy. This crucial aspect of emotional intelligence has nothing to do with being nice or placating people. It has a whole lot more to do with knowing how to treat people according to their emotional reactions. Someone with real empathy can see those reactions and make decisions based on what's going in the lives of other people.

EMPATHY MEANS LISTENING

An empathetic leader has good listening skills and really hears what people say. Listening skills can be developed with some simple techniques—I teach workshops on this to my corporate clients. They tell me afterward that the skills truly help them communicate better.

In my workshops and with my individual clients, I teach active listening skills—conversational techniques that keep communications open and avoid roadblocks and misunderstanding. Active listening skills reflect back to the speaker what you understand and how you think the speaker feels. Active listening is a communications skill that involves not just listening to the words people say but also to the things they don't say.

I teach my clients the therapist hypothesis. This is the belief that the capacity for self-insight, problem solving, and growth resides primarily in the speaker. This means that the central questions for the listener are not, "What I can do for this person?" or even "How do I see this person?"

The questions are rather, "How does this person see themselves and their situation?"

One valuable tool for better listening is repeating back to the person what they said but in a different way. So if an employee says to you, "I'll have the report ready tomorrow," you can reply, "So it sounds like by tomorrow you'll have the report ready." That lets the employee know that you heard what was said and you're in agreement with it.

I teach some basic ground rules for good listening:

- Don't interrupt.
- Don't change the subject or move in a new direction until you've been directed to.
- Don't rehearse in your own head what you're going to say.
- Don't interrogate.
- Don't teach.
- Don't give advice.

Use polite phrases that show respect in the interaction.

- Mr., Mrs., or Miss as appropriate
- Excuse me …
- Pardon me …
- May I suggest …
- Let's focus on …
- Would you please …

"Please" and "Thank you" go a long way in easing tension and helping develop a positive connection.

Active listening is about being attentive and interested, not distracted. You create a positive atmosphere through nonverbal behavior. Allow the speaker to bounce ideas and feelings off of you while assuming a nonjudgmental, noncritical manner. Don't ask a lot of questions. You don't want people to feel you're grilling them like an attorney in a courtroom.

Three main types of questions can keep the conversation moving in a positive direction:

- Leading: "Would you like to talk about …?" "Could you tell me more about that?"
- Open-ended: "Who/What/Where/When/How?"
- Reflective: "It sounds like you …" or, "In other words …"

The goal is to let the speaker know you're listening—your questions are just to make sure you understand.

Once you've asked the questions, listen carefully to the answers— focus on the individual speaking to you. Pay attention to the inter-action and show empathy. Don't discount the speaker's feelings or patronize her by saying, "That's not that bad," or "You'll feel better tomorrow."

Indicate you're listening by providing noncommittal responses, such as, "I see," or "Uh-huh." Give nonverbal acknowledgement by head nodding, but don't do that too much.

If you nod all the time, that's also a way of saying, "You're boring me to tears. When are you going to be finished?" Try to mirror the speaker or the employee with open and relaxed nonverbal body expressions, eye contact, and so on.

Invite them to say more by using phrases such as, "I'd like to hear more about that."

As a leader, sometimes your goal is just to listen and express empathy, warmth, and positive regard and not to necessarily fix the situation. Often, people need to just be heard. They have the answer within themselves. It's not necessarily your job to give them the answer. By providing an opportunity for people to talk through their problem or their issue, you help clarify their thinking as well as provide the necessary emotional release. Active listening facilitates problem solving. As the French philosopher Blaise Pascal said, "People are generally better persuaded by the reasons they have themselves discovered than by those that enter the minds of others." If we let our employees or leaders come up with their own decisions, then that answer is going to come from within them. They're going to come to the conclusion you most likely want them to come to anyway.

AVOIDING BURNOUT: EMPATHY AND REALITY

Burnout means emotional, mental, and physical exhaustion caused by excessive and prolonged stress. One very common symptom of burnout is diminished interest in work.

Leaders who are high in empathy can burn out. Their empathy gets to be a little too much—they get into fix mode. If you have empathy and use that to get to the solution the employee wants, then you'll be fine. But if you decide to fix things and they don't get fixed the way you want them to, then that's when you get into burnout. You work really hard, and yet the results aren't what you aimed for. That's frustrating, exhausting, and stressful—all the ingredients to make you feel burned out and uninterested in anything, especially your work.

Codependency—excessive emotional reliance on a partner—is a major cause of burnout. It's toxic and can create a lot of the negative stress that leads to burnout. It's likely to happen if you're trying to get people to do what you want them to do, as opposed to allowing them to find their own way.

Codependency usually refers to personal relationships, but the concept applies to business as well. One of my clients is the president of a company. He became extremely codependent about feeling responsible for his employees. He felt so responsible that he was always worrying about them, to the point where he couldn't be objective. He would think, "My manager is having another baby. Maybe I should give him another raise because his wife now stays home with the kids." That's codependence, because the manager is the one who decided to have a child and already knows how to manage his money. He doesn't need his boss to tell him that. It also opens the boss to accusations of favoritism and unequal treatment.

If you find yourself going down the codependency path, you can pull back before it does real damage. I recommend an excellent book called *The Language of Letting Go,* by Melody Beattie. The book was written for people who have addicts and alcoholics in their lives, but it also works with any type of codependence. An organization called Co-Dependents Anonymous (www.coda.org) can also be very helpful.

Case Study:
Improving Empathy

Empathy is a crucial tool for good leadership. I was able to demonstrate this for the leadership team at a large auto dealership by having the team members do some role playing.

We set the scene with one of the team members playing the manager and me playing a team member employee with a problem. The goal was to see how empathetic the manager could be. Here's how the dialogue went.

Team member (me): I've had a tough time the past few months. My divorce, sharing custody of the kids, my finances, moving to a new place—I really feel I need a month off to get back on track.

Manager: Wow, I didn't know that was going in your life. Sure, go ahead, take time off, recuperate, and get back to us when you can.

The manager then pushed back his chair, signaling he was done with playing the role. His body language clearly displayed he was happy with his response.

I asked the group, "Did this manager connect to the reality of the employee's problems?"

A heated discussion ensued among the team. The consensus was that he spoke from the manager's shoes, not the team member's shoes. We talked a lot about what empathy really is. When we did the exercise again with two new volunteers, the dialogue was very different.

Team member: I've had a tough time the past few months. My divorce, sharing custody of the kids, my finances, moving to a new place—I really feel I need a month off to get back on track.

Manager: I see you're really upset over your divorce. I understand what you're going through and why you feel you need some time off. I can give you 15 days off to rest, recuperate, and not worry about things here. Who would you recommend from the team to take on some of your responsibilities while you're away? What they can't do, I'll take care of. Let me know if I can help with anything else.

The group learned that empathy is the ability to abandon our own reality and enter into that of another when the situation calls for it. Empathy as a leadership characteristic isn't about just nodding and saying "I understand." It is truly understanding the view of the other person and having a sense of what it's like to be in their world. This is why EQ training is a must for managers. High EQ is the key to good interpersonal relationships.

In this case, the leader balanced his empathy for the employee with empathy for the entire team and the needs of the business. He was able to give the employee some time off but only 15 days instead of 30. In this way, he achieved the balance he knew was required while being an empathetic leader.

I like to quote Daniel H. Pink, author of *Drive: The Surprising Truth About What Motivates Us:* Empathy is about standing in someone else's shoes, feeling with his or her heart, seeing with his or her eyes. Not only is empathy hard to outsource and automate, but it also makes the world a better place.

CHAPTER 10

Social Skills for Leadership

Good leaders are socially aware; they're responsive to the people around them. They motivate them and build good teams. They're high in the social skills aspect of emotional intelligence.

Leaders with good social skills can easily find common ground with their team. They're able to build good rapport within the team as well as outside the company through networking. They're generally good at building rapport with the chief of the company. Usually, people with high social skills are great at persuasion. They listen openly and send convincing messages. They negotiate and dissolve disagreements. They're good at inspiring individuals as well as groups. They're very good at initiating or managing change. They're good at nurturing instrumental relationships for building further bonds and working with others toward shared goals. Most importantly, they create good group synergy.

Leaders who are high in social skills don't allow bullying or abusive behavior within their departments. Unfortunately, when a leader isn't high in self-awareness and self-regulation, abusive behavior can be a workplace problem. For employees who have to deal with this, I advise not taking it personally—imagine yourself wearing a suit of armor when dealing with the abusive person. Don't let his or her negativity affect you to the point where you start having negative self-talk. You can't change the person, so you have to change the way you react to them—while also bringing the issue to the attention of the people above you or to the human resources department. In the worst-case scenario, it may be time to hit the road.

INCREASING YOUR SOCIAL SKILLS

Some people, especially introverts, are uncomfortable in social situations and networking. They feel they don't know who to talk to or what to say. They're uncomfortable approaching people they don't know. I encourage these people to attend lots of industry and community events as a way to practice their skills. To lessen the stress, I tell them to get to the event right on time or even early. Have your nametag prepared in advance, because often a lack of preparation makes these situations more stressful. Have your business cards ready in your pocket so you can just reach in to quickly grasp one. All the preparation keeps you from feeling you're juggling or floundering. I advise people to find someone in the room who also looks uncomfortable and talk to that person. Suddenly, you're helping someone—and any time you're helping somebody, you're going to feel better. For my introvert clients, I recommend an excellent book called *Net-*

working for People Who Hate Networking: A Field Guide for Introverts, the Overwhelmed, and the Underconnected, by Devora Zack.

If your social skills are on the low side, work on your friendships. Bond with people one at a time. The quality of your relationships is more important than the quantity.

At work, help your teammates. That forces you to interact positively while doing something you know about. Your interaction is going to be successful, and your coworkers will be grateful to you.

One of the very best ways to improve your social skills is to join some kind of special interest group, community group, or professional association that meets regularly. That's a great way to network and develop professional bonds. I recommend your local branch of Toastmasters or Business Network International, but really any organization is a good choice.

Case Study:
Warren B. Learns to Listen

I coach Warren B., a very high producer in the financial industry. He was so busy he brought in a junior associate named Joan M. They would go meet with potential clients, and afterward he would think the meeting went very well. Joan would agree the meeting went well but also point out that he was so busy talking that he wasn't hearing what the client said, so he missed opportunities. After she had brought it to his attention several times, Warren decided she was right. He didn't know how to fix himself, so he came to me.

We worked together once a week for about six months. On his EQ assessment he came out low on empathy, so we worked on that. I would have Warren, who was very wealthy, sit in a park and watch homeless people and try to imagine he was one of them. I had him journal about the experience. It really helped him develop more empathy in general.

We also worked on his active listening. He needed the most help dealing with introverts, who tend to think before they speak and may let long pauses come into the conversation. As an extrovert, this drove Warren crazy. I would say something to him, and I would stop midsentence, and he would have to wait on me to finish. And I would fidget, and I would squirm, and when he would start talking and interrupt me, I'd clap my hands.

Soon he realized that every time he interrupted, he was going to be in trouble. And he stopped it.

Warren learned to listen and ask the right empathetic questions to build trust with potential clients. He learned to meet with millionaires and not talk about money or sell them at all—he would ask about their grandchildren, their hobbies, their interests, and just listen all through lunch. At the end of the meal, his investors would often hand over the check and say, "By the way, this was our best meeting ever." And all he had done was listen.

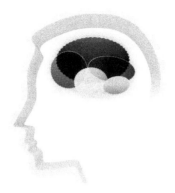

CHAPTER 11

Leadership Issues for Women

Women often face more challenging issues as they learn to lead. At the same time, women have a slight edge over men in EQ because they're more empathetic. Women leaders are more persuasive and better at team building, yet women in leadership positions are more prone to depression. Building your EQ skills can be a big help in getting past structural barriers to achieve a better level of success.

THE CHALLENGES

The world has changed. Today, women have more potential to move up in leadership. However, there are many organizations and cultures where very few women are in the upper, upper, upper levels of a company. A national accounting firm only recently named a female CEO—the first in this industry. The lack of female executives in the tech industry is well known. And women even at high levels are still a step behind on salary. That's particularly sad when you look at all the extra value women bring—more empathy, better team-building skills, and oftentimes more motivation.

SELF-SABOTAGING BEHAVIOR

Women leaders can self-sabotage by not bonding with other women. In my coaching, I've seen among women at a certain level there's a lot of jealousy and pettiness, rather than collegiality.

I've seen situations where two women in an organization were both in the running for an upper leadership position. They didn't help each other; in fact, they made it more difficult. Men will battle it out and then hug each other. Women battle it out, and then they flip each other off. They sometimes make it difficult for themselves.

Sometimes, women have fought so hard to get where they are that they've lost track of their original purpose. They think, *I got here by myself without much help*, which is often true, especially for older women. They don't realize the power in being able to help the people coming up behind them. But you can't pull up the ladder behind you. You need to extend a helping hand. Also, mentoring somebody or taking on an intern keeps you on your A-game. Why not open up the door to somebody?

STRUCTURAL ISSUES AND CORPORATE CULTURE

The genuine barriers to women advancing to leadership positions are structural and corporate. Upper management tends to think, *Oh, she's a woman. She's going to be more emotional, and she's not going to be able to stand up to the good ol' boys.* That's not true. In fact, women are more persuasive, more encouraging, and actually can get more things done by using their empathetic ways because they express things differently. They're better at it, but in a good ol' boys network, it's not viewed that way. When a company prefers to promote from within, and the higher ranks are filled mostly by men, women have a harder time getting noticed. These companies don't make a genuine effort to bring diversity to the leadership by looking beyond their immediate staff. Today, larger corporations have very defined ways of trying to increase their diversity by insisting that searches go beyond the company or within the narrower top executive circle. They're making greater effort. Of course, it doesn't mean that in the end their hiring decision is any different, but at least they're expanding the search.

Old attitudes are still around and are major structural barriers. When a little boy is growing up and he's assertive, people say, "He's going to be a real leader."

When a little girl is assertive, people say, "Boy is she bossy."

When you label somebody bossy, that's like saying, "Don't do that. Don't speak up." As these girls grow up, they're stifled. When they do speak up in the workplace, they're called bitchy, not assertive. They get a lot of very confusing mixed messages from coworkers and the people above them.

In addition to the structural barriers, women striving for leadership often lack mentors. It's hard to find female mentors willing to work with younger women. At a recent Chamber of Commerce event in my region, I looked around and saw that there were probably a thousand people there. I thought, *If I was here looking for a woman mentor, would I fine a good one here?* To be honest, I'm not sure I would have found one—women were in a definite minority. Some of my female coaching clients have had a lot of trouble finding a woman willing to mentor them. Mentoring is time consuming—I know, because I mentor several young women. But it's also very beneficial for both sides.

I coach a lot of women who are rising through the ranks, and I know that becoming a successful female leader is difficult. I strongly recommend an excellent book called *Making It in Corporate America: How Women Can Survive, Prosper and Make a Difference,* by Diane Smallen-Grob.

THE VALUE OF FEMININE EQ

You're a woman with exactly the same credentials as your male counterpart. When it comes to moving up into leadership, you're equal in IQ, but as a woman, you may have the EQ edge. Since you're probably better in the five areas of EQ, you're going to shine more, although a man, simply by being a man, may seem to have an edge on you. But if you as a woman are more emotionally stable or intelligent, then you have the real edge, because in leadership that's the key. It's not necessarily IQ, it's EQ.

The best female leaders, like the best male leaders, are strong in all EQ areas. You might have a lot of empathy, for instance, but unless that's also balanced by the other qualities, you'll be a doormat—a real pushover.

Because they're good at empathy, women leaders are more persuasive and they're better at team building. They tend toward a leadership style that's collaborative and uses interpersonal skills, rather than one that's based on dominance, position, and power. That's why women tend to be more effective. They can implement teamwork better because they will involve and motivate more people.

Women in leadership positions need a thick skin. People don't have to like you. In fact, being a leader means that sometimes people aren't going to like you. As a woman, you're probably more empathetic than a man in a similar position. When you have good empathy, it lets you appreciate where the person who dislikes you is coming from. That's where EQ can help. If you're self-aware, then you can understand the other person and deal with the reality that some people won't like you by not taking it personally or doubting yourself.

We know from studies that women in leadership positions are more prone to depression. I think it has a lot to do with juggling a marriage or relationship and sometimes children. They're juggling a whole lot more than a man has to—because society as a whole has not given up on the mom being the primary caregiver. When a woman moves into a high leadership position, it puts even more stress on her. The more emotionally intelligent you are, the easier it's going to be to handle those stressors.

One of my personal heroes is Eleanor Roosevelt. She's a great role model for leadership. Years in the public eye at a time when women were far less visible taught her a lot about surviving and thriving. I'm sharing the quotes below, which have been attributed to her, because this wisdom applies equally well to women in the workplace:

> You cannot take anything personally.

> You cannot bear grudges.

> You must finish the day's work when the day's work is done.

You cannot get discouraged too easily.

You have to take defeat over and over again and pick up and go on.

Be sure of your facts.

Argue the other side with a friend until you have found the answer to every point that might be brought up against you.

Women who are willing to be leaders must stand out and be shot at.

More and more they're going to do it and more and more they should do it.

Every woman in public life needs to develop skin as tough as a rhinoceros hide.

USING YOUR FEMININE EQ
IN THE WORKPLACE

Just because you're a woman and are naturally a bit more empathetic than a man doesn't mean you're exceptionally high in empathy. In my experience, male or female, you can't be too high in empathy. I once had a client who had the highest empathy I ever saw. She came out at 8.7 out of 10 on her EQ assessment. It was clear from her assessment that she had a unique skill of treating people according to their emotional reactions. She was very good at utilizing this information when making decisions. Even so, she had an area to work on: fully understanding others before communicating her point of view.

Until you reach 10 on the assessment (none of my clients ever have), it's still possible to sharpen your skills.

Empathy is a great skill in a leader, as long as it doesn't invite sympathy and as long as you don't become codependent or set your boundaries too low. I think boundaries are an area where women as a whole can tend to get in trouble. When their boundaries aren't high or clear enough, people overstep them, and then there are problems. But in fact, when boundaries are clearly and appropriately set, people generally will not overstep.

I advise my female clients to use the sandwich method when you have to tell someone about a boundary problem. Give the initial input by starting with a piece of bread—something fluffy. If the issue is a dispute between two employees that wasn't brought to your attention, "I understand that you're upset about this interaction and probably rightfully so."

Then you give them the meat, "In the future I would like to see you handle it a little differently and maybe approach me about taking charge of it before you say anything."

Then you end with another piece of fluffy bread so that way you send them away feeling good. Say something like, "However I do appreciate your concern about this company and your showing an interest in how everyone gets along." The sandwich method lets you be empathetic, yet it's still taking charge and setting a boundary of what you expect in the future. Particularly with women, if we don't tell people what to expect in the future, they think, *What I did is acceptable*, when in fact it wasn't.

For a lot of women, it's hard to be the boss because you want all your employees to also be your friends and like you. As a leader, you're just not going to have everybody like you. It's just like the president.

Some people like him, and some people don't. When you're a leader, you're setting yourself up for people that probably don't like you. Part of being a leader is not being popular but doing what's right for the greater cause and for the mission. Once you accept that, leading is easier.

I teach my female clients the JADE technique. Once you've stated your case you don't have to Justify it, you don't have to Argue about it, you don't have to Defend it, and you don't have to Explain it. You're the boss. You said it, and that should be enough.

From an EQ perspective, female leaders need a high level of self-awareness to help them grow a thicker skin. If your self-awareness is low, typically you're worried about what other people are thinking or what they're saying. You forget that you're doing nothing wrong and that people are just going to talk about you no matter what you do. It's hard to get past being sensitive about criticism and negative responses. I'm real sensitive, and it is very difficult. I can be in the middle of a presentation and see that everybody's loving it—except for one person. The person with the frown on her face is the only person I see. I immediately think she's sitting there wishing I'd just shut up and leave.

I gave a talk to a group of women business owners one December about de-stressing for the holidays. One woman in the audience made faces during the whole presentation. I was already a bit nervous about the presentation. This woman, who was tall, lean, and beautiful, was looking at me up and down, and I was thinking, *Oh, dear God*. Then I remembered not to get wrapped up with feeling judged.

I thought, *Who knows, maybe her dog died*.

At the end of the presentation she came up to me, and she said, "Where do I sign up for coaching?"

I thought, *Isn't it amazing that what I think is going on in her head is nothing close to what's going on in her head?* What she was doing was processing all the things in her life that weren't congruent with what I was talking about.

As women, we tend to think it has something to do with us. It has nothing to do with us and everything to do with them. And even if it does have something to do with us, it's none of our business what other people think. We can't do anything about it anyway.

HANDLING CRITICISM

When you're criticized, the best thing to do is to just say, "Thank you for the input. I will certainly consider that." Don't respond beyond that. Walk away and process. If you totally disagree with it, ask three trusted friends if they think it's true.

If it's not true, then assume that this is just one person who reads your actions that way. If the criticism affects your job, then you take it seriously and make changes. But if it doesn't, then just go about your business and forget it. That's where the EQ skills of self-awareness and self-regulation come in. When somebody's criticizing you, self-regulation lets you be brave enough to just stand there and take it and say, "Oh, you may be right," or to just let it go. It's hard not to get defensive in a situation like that, but that's probably the worst thing you can do. Self-awareness will help you stay calm and objective.

Case Study:
Measuring Up

Marsha B. became my client after she was made the first female CEO of a large hospital. She was stepping into the shoes of the successful male executive who was now her boss. Needless to say, that was a little daunting, but what complicated the situation more was that the hospital environment had changed quickly over the past few years.

Marsha kept trying to match or even beat her predecessor's numbers in an environment that made it nearly impossible to do so. Everyone told her this was just the new reality, but Marsha didn't want to see it that way. She felt that as the first woman in the job, and as someone without an MBA degree, she had to do better. After enough long hours and lost sleep, she came to me for coaching.

We discussed the issues, including her feeling that as a woman she had something to prove. Marsha realized she needed to talk to her boss and get his perspective. After enough coaching, she finally got up the nerve to talk to him—and he told her he knew things were changing fast and that every hospital was having the same problem she was regarding meeting their previous numbers. He assured her that she was doing really well. It took more coaching to get Marsha to really believe that he meant it and that despite her being a woman without an advanced degree, she was doing a great job.

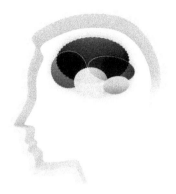

CHAPTER 12

True Leadership

Your EQ skills as a leader can help you create a collaborative, harmonious, and profitable workplace. And, just as importantly, you will be a more effective—and happier—leader.

Any leader who scores on the high end of an EQ assessment is going to be a far better leader than one who does not. If you are such a person, you will have what it takes to go from good to great. You're going to have a more positive attitude. You're going to be a better motivator. You're going to lead by example. You'll have no problem picking a team with skills that enhance yours and those of your employees. You won't feel threatened when your staff has skills you don't; rather, you will rely on their expertise and applaud their achievements.

Leaders with lower EQ rarely hire anyone smarter or more talented than they are, because they might feel threatened. Their self-awareness isn't strong enough to understand and overcome this, so they hire beneath them. A leader who can venture out and reach beyond his or her comfort zone is the one who's going to put together the best team.

A leader with high EQ is also somebody who's going to say what she means and mean what she says. She's not worried about just making friends. She's concerned with persuading and motivating and influencing the team to be the best they can be. Leaders who do that are trusted, and with that trust comes credibility and consistency. Good leaders are extremely consistent.

A leader high in EQ is somebody who's going to empower, not overpower, others. Empowerment is key to personal and professional success for team members. What matters more than a leader's knowledge or experience is how he influences the team and empowers individuals to rise to the occasion by giving them that chance to excel.

I'm still in touch with a young woman who once interned for me. She told me that I made a big impact on her life because she was an introvert like me, and she had learned from watching me to embrace that part of herself. I had empowered her by showing her an introvert can still be a good presenter and a people person. I helped her learn to honor herself and to be who she is. I'm very proud that she has moved on to a high-level position in hospital management.

If you can give power to the people you lead wherever possible, they'll achieve more. Give them the power to excel and to be the best they can be; and they will.

John Maxwell, my favorite guru on management, says that a good leader will do anything for his people, because they'll do anything for him. He says, "My team makes me better than I am. My team multiplies my value to others. My team enables me to do what I do best. My team gives me more time. My team represents me where I could not go. My team provides community for our enjoyment. My team fulfills the desires of my heart." If your team is doing all that, then you're a good, if not great, leader. And they are able to do that because you empower them.

TEAM CONFLICTS

No matter how cohesive your team is, conflict will occur. As a leader, your attitude and how you respond to conflict will help resolve issues quickly and keep everybody collaborating. Consistency is key here.

Leaders who are high in self-regulation tend to have a good attitude when they're resolving conflict. They don't fly off the handle. They sandwich their critique of the conflict by bringing both parties in, listening attentively to both parties' sides, and then finding a solution. A good leader makes it clear that once the conflict has been resolved, all the team members are still valued, that they are expected to flourish from this point forward, and that the issue need never be brought up again.

If the conflict does come up again, a good leader tries to understand why. Bring together the people that are involved for a discussion. A good starting line is, "Tell me what's going on, because I thought we had addressed that." Let everyone speak his peace again, because obviously it wasn't resolved the last time. The point is for the leader to have good self-regulation and not react negatively or angrily. If there needs to be some sort of reprimand or penalty, being calm and even-handed makes people more accepting of your decision. Move forward from there; learn from it and don't dwell.

In some situations, the true leader recognizes that something is beyond his capacity and outside help is needed. This is when it can be very helpful to say, "Let's address this. Let's get you a coach to work on this. Maybe you have some stuff going on that you'd like to share with a coach in private." A leader can be so heavily invested in a project or group of people that he may be too close for an unbiased perspective. No matter how wonderful he is, having an outside view may be what is most needed.

One of my corporate clients sent a manager to me for coaching. He told me in advance, "He's going to con you. He's going to make you think he's doing everything right when, in fact, he's not."

I've been doing this for a long time, so it's pretty hard to con me. I approached the manager with the idea of looking to see what he was doing right, not wrong, and that's where we began. Most clients want to please their coach. He listed several things he felt were his strengths. I applauded those strengths, and we talked about what an impact those strengths make on the whole organization, and then toward the end of the session, once we had built strong rapport, I asked, "What do you think you could improve on?"

He hesitated. I reminded him that I can't discuss or repeat what my clients tell me, and then he quickly named two things he felt he could work on. I firmly believe because we had such good rapport, he put his trust in me and was ready to change some things. He shared with me at the end of the session, "My boss said we would really hit it off." He then added, "My boss must really care about me to allow me to come see you because I take time away from the office and I'm sure it's not cheap." I assured him that he was worth the investment, and when he left my office that day he had a bounce in his step that he hadn't had when he arrived.

After several months of coaching him, this manager took the EQ assessment and was able to see in print some additional things he needed to work on. He's been growing and shining ever since.

SELF-REGULATION: MASTERING YOUR EMOTIONS

Leaders often ask themselves, "Have I mastered my emotions, or am I mastered by them?" If you're mastered by your emotions, then you're probably not doing a good job of leading. But if you've mastered your emotions and you've got them under control, then you're being a good leader. As part of questioning yourself, ask yourself, "Am I willing to do what it takes today for the good of the team?"

EXPANDING YOUR SKILLS

A good way for a leader to help the team is by continuing to learn and expand his own education and skills. By taking additional courses on leadership or management or people skills or presentation skills or any of those types of things, you show the team you're interested in being better and are willing to put in the effort to grow. Then they want to grow and be better as well.

I recommend finding a mentor, even if it's just a temporary arrangement. The best way to grow is by having a mentor or coach to hold you accountable and help you improve. Professional athletes have coaches. In fact, they would never dream of playing their sport without a coach. Not only do they have a main coach, but they have coaches for specific skills and for training. It's the same for anyone striving for excellence. I believe that people who don't ask for help are limiting themselves. The more we can open up to the world and rely on the world, the healthier and more whole we're going to be, because we all need everybody.

I coach a lot of mastermind groups—smart people who meet regularly to network, advise, and help each other. I find that when people meet with groups of their peers, just listening to the other people and how they've done things and how they failed at things could save someone from making the same mistakes. A group has a lot of power to motivate change. In mastermind groups, I often ask the participants, "What positive improvements can you make today, based on your understanding of how you can fit within your area, organization, market, or industry?" I guarantee, by being in a group, you'll find out something useful. You'll learn about some type of improvement you can make.

Case Study: Managing Conflict

I coach all the managers at a big company. One of them, Richard P., gets really annoyed when other managers and teammates are sloppy on details. Because they forget the details, they make his job harder, and he screams at them. He was constantly peevish about it and complained to the president, "Here's what's happening, and nobody's doing their jobs." I worked with him for six months to teach him better self-regulation and empathy.

Richard needed to see the problem from the other side. Everyone is overworked, and details just sometimes slip by—it's not a personal attack on him. Today, when someone doesn't give him what he needs, he very calmly goes to the person that did the paperwork and says, "I'm sure you didn't mean this, but unfortunately I'm missing this one line of information. Can we please get this right now, because I have a client in front of me, and I need it?"

His EQ training helped him in other areas of his work and life as well. He not only gets along better with his colleagues, but his wife has also told me that he's much easier to live with. He shows empathy toward her at the end of a bad workday, he pitches in more at home, and, is open to trying other activities that she's tried to get him to try for years.

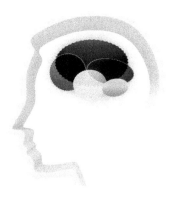

Conclusion

CHOOSING YOUR COACH

Thank you for reading my book. I hope it has been helpful to you and that you have learned some ways to better your personal and professional life. The stories I've included are about the clients I've helped over the years. They have shared with me that training them in better leadership and EQ skills has changed their lives both professionally and personally.

When my clients change things for the better in their personal lives, their professional lives get better, too. Things go better at work, they get raises, and often they get big promotions. Most importantly, they become better leaders.

Sometimes, I hear about the changes directly from the clients or their bosses, but sometimes the route is more indirect. I'll give you an example of this now in my final story.

Recently, I was at a conference, and a woman came up to me. I had no clue who she was. She said, "Thank you."

I said, "You're welcome, but I'm sorry—I don't know who you are."

She replied, "You worked with my boss Bill K. last year."

In working with Bill, we had talked a lot about his relationship with his business partner. Bill wasn't showing much leadership in the firm. He was letting his partner take the lead, which was causing friction. His EQ assessment showed that he needed to develop his listening skills and better self-awareness. When he did, he was able to share his thoughts more with his partner and avoid procrastinating. Suddenly, the staff meetings were going more smoothly. Things were getting done. Things that had been issues for years and years were getting addressed. His partner was even more motivated, because he felt less pressure to be doing all the work and making all the decisions. EQ training made all the difference not just to Bill but also to his partner and his employees. The improvement in morale and motivation at the company is why someone I never met was thanking me for my help.

When you decide that better leadership skills or a better personal or professional life is what you want, the first step is awareness. The second step is to make that call or send that email to an experienced coach whom you feel comfortable with. The key in selecting a coach is to find someone who has insight into your issues, is trained in coaching techniques, is a good listener, and can help guide you through the process.

A lot of my clients say they picked me because I walk the walk and talk the talk. I've asked them how they know this, and often they know someone who knows me and trusts me, or they've been told that the things I ask of clients, I always practice myself. I guess people really do "watch us when we don't know they're watching." A coach doesn't have to be in your geographic area—in fact, most coaches are readily available on the phone and through Skype. Reach out to a coach today. The longer you put it off, the more you're putting off having additional money in your pocket and a happier life.

Feel free to reach out to me at www.CoachingByKarenNutter.com with your coaching questions. I'd love to hear from you and get feedback. I'm always interested in talking to individuals and companies about leadership, teamwork, and ways to use emotional intelligence to improve and move forward both personally and professionally.

Printed in the USA
CPSIA information can be obtained
at www.ICGtesting.com
JSHW012036140824
68134JS00033B/3093

9 781599 326030